"It's not every day that a bartender creates a drink aesthetic so wholly unique that you know it when you see it. Natasha David has not just created an aesthetic, but an entire world. Her influence helped make the apéritif a part of modern American drinking culture, but on new terms (more whimsy, more glitter). *Drink Lightly* manages to be both an imaginative, Technicolor portal into her world and an essential manual for building a better low-ABV cocktail."

—TALIA BAIOCCHI, editor in chief, Punch

"Expert mixologist Natasha David's *Drink Lightly* is absolutely genius for anyone who loves the balance, elegance, and flavors of classic cocktails yet is looking for a low-ABV version. I'm grateful this book exists to help me navigate my home bar in a new way, and especially because it comes with a garnish of disco!"

—DANA COWIN, founder of *Speaking Broadly*

"For Natasha David a disco ball isn't optional, it's essential. And it's through that vortex of glittery illumination that *Drink Lightly* takes flight. David has never met a classic cocktail spec that can't be elevated by promoting sherry, white port, or aromatized wine from demure modifier to shining star. Her confidence, grace, ever-present whimsy, and hard-earned wisdom are the keys to unlocking the secrets of good taste, and a good time."

—BRAD THOMAS PARSONS, author of *Bitters, Amaro,* and *Last Call*

DRINK LIGHTLY

NATASHA DAVID

Photographs by Kristin Teig

Illustrations by Andrés Yeah

Clarkson Potter/Publishers
New York

LIGHTLY

LIGHTLY

LIGHTLY

DRINK LIGHTLY

DRINK LIGHTLY

DRINK LIGHTLY

A Lighter Take on Serious Cocktails, with 100+ Recipes for Low- and No-Alcohol Drinks

For Elliot and Lola
Made entirely possible by Jeremy

Contents

GULPABLE THIRST QUENCHERS

Refreshing, tart, and ultra-lighthearted

SLOW SIPPERS

Soulful and silky

164 DECADENT TREATS
Lush, indulgent, and gratifying

196 PARTY STARTERS
Invigorating bowls of shareable pleasure

226 THE CELEBRATION NEVER STOPS
Alcohol-free drinks for a good time, anytime

FOREWORD

Even after years of tending bar and thinking far too deeply about cocktails, to this day I find myself fascinated by the mystique of a talented bartender—how they can grab a handful of bottles from a back bar, pour a few carefully measured splashes into a shaker or mixing glass, and out the other end comes a beautiful, perfect drink. It's no less than magic, a sorcery I've spent an entire career trying to decode.

And yet, despite this fascination, there have been times when I've hit the wall of frustration with cocktails. Be it my own creative block or malaise with trend upon trend upon trend, I'd be lying if I didn't look in the mirror frequently and prophetically ask, "Who cares? It's just cold booze in a glass." For a guy whose life revolves around cocktails in one way or another, not a great place to be. It was in just this state that Natasha David came into my world.

After knowing each other peripherally for years, we finally worked together at a bar in lower Manhattan, a highly aspiration cocktail lounge full of hubris and questionable decisions, eventually succumbed to the floods of Hurricane Sandy. I had found myself deeply impressed by Natasha's grace behind that bar, her gentle hospitality with guests, a stunning level of execution, and a complete and unquestionable ability to bartend circles around everyone. I remember a moment as if it were yesterday: sitting midway at the bar casually talking to a friend but really watching Natasha work, thinking *I wanna work with this person forever*. Beat down as I was by the project (it was rough!), I nevertheless felt renewed and inspired in that moment.

After the dust had settled on that bar, my partner David Kaplan and I found ourselves with a great opportunity: a ridiculously tiny raw space on the Lower East Side begging to be a dark, moody cocktail bar. We had endless ideas on how it would look, how it would feel when you walked down the stairs, how it would push cocktail culture in a new direction. But we lived on the other side of the country at the time and knew we needed not only someone to be the bar's day-to-day, but also a partner who could infuse their life and soul into the place. Natasha was without question our first choice, and to our elation (and relief!), she agreed to come on board.

Building and opening a bar is no less than thrilling, but you must love it in a way only a masochist can. I've built a lot of bars; it's my drug of choice. But damn if the opening of what would become Nitecap wasn't brutal: construction delays, permitting issues, dealing with the delightful folks at ConEd, strapped for cash at every turn—I understand why some people aren't built for it. Amid this, we found respite and motivation in plotting and planning how Nitecap would shed the conventional wisdom of a cocktail bar and be both fun *and* aspirational, a novel concept at the time. Months and months of brainstorming, writing, thinking, designing, and arguing, finally we started work on the menu. Natasha came to L.A. as a retreat of sorts, and I had every intention of taking lead on creating drinks with her, guiding the process. She didn't need a guide.

We had set aside a week to design and craft the menu, and as we started tinkering with ideas, it became clear that all the skills I had previously seen Natasha perform behind a bar were a shiny façade for what she truly possessed. As she and my partner Devon Tarby shaped ideas into finished drinks, I recessed more and more in the background, in awe of what I was seeing and tasting. Within each of Natasha's cocktails was a narrative, a grounding in some aspect of nostalgia or cultural inspiration that wasn't superficial—these cocktails meant something to her, they represented her past, her present, her future. Much like any great artist, they were the sum of both the context of her perspective of the world and her life's biography. To this day, I'm wowed by how revolutionary that is for cocktail creators, and I will forever coach bartenders to seek it in their own work.

It took many years of enjoying Natasha's cocktails and having a front row seat to her creativity to understand that for her, cocktails do not live in an isolated, intellectualized realm. They are entwined with the rhythm of her life, the evolution from actor to bartender to bar owner to mother—and all garnished with a cheeky sprinkle of glitter and a conviction to make the world a better place. They are undoubtedly delicious, but they also reflect a greater perspective on life: that we should enjoy the great things that the universe gives us, because joy *is* nourishment. Years after Nitecap first opened, I think back on those early menu development days (and the many versions that followed over the proceeding years) as pivotal in shaping my own greater appreciation of life—both inside and outside of bars.

For me, page after page of this book felt like a walk down memory lane, times I count as some of the best in my life. *Drink Lightly*

reminds me that cocktails (or anything in life) do not form in a vacuum—they are intertwined with the circumstances and challenges of life and the complexities of evolving one's passions, the struggles of balancing life, art, business, and family—and that knowing those details allows us to love a cocktail even more, to understand its beauty more deeply. And so, within the pages that follow, you'll not only have a bevy of delicious cocktail recipes to explore, you'll also understand more about the *why* and *how* they came to be. I hope this deepens your enjoyment and inspires your own creativity.

As you wade in and find yourself inevitably praying at the Alter of the Spritz, please also heed Natasha's advice—both literally and existentially. The one thing I love most about her cocktails is that they are are more than just delicious, cold liquid. Each one is a valuable lesson in technique, a master class in demystifying flavor combinations, and a call to action for all of us to explore ideas outside our comfort zone.

But more than anything, this book underscores the value in laughing just a little bit louder and a whole lot longer. Because after all, joy is the greatest cocktail garnish there is.

Cheers!

Alex Day
Partner, Death & Co; author of *Death & Co: Modern Classic Cocktails; Cocktail Codex: Fundamentals, Formulas, Evolutions; Death & Co Welcome Home*

Portland, Maine
Written while drinking a spritz and a side of fries

WHAT YOU'RE GETTING YOURSELF INTO:

COCKTAILS AS JOY

THE ELUSIVE APÉRITIF. A STYLE OF DRINKING DRENCHED IN TRADITION AND HISTORY YET SOMEHOW COMPLETELY EFFORTLESS AND TIMELESS.

It's a cocktail that encourages interaction and thoughtful debate, that lifts the spirits or comforts a broken heart. It is a tumbler joyfully overflowing and topped with a plump and juicy orange slice. But in my world, it can be even more. It's a blank canvas full of uncharted opportunity. These recipes go beyond the "something bitter plus soda" paradigm and take full advantage of the incredible and vast array of low-proof spirits, liqueurs, and wines. (And, yes, I've also included some carefully considered cocktails without booze because they too deserve attention and care.) My drinks are rooted in classic cocktail structure, meaning they are modeled after those timeless recipes we all trust and love, and are inspired by memories, emotions, and places; but above all, they're grounded in a deep-seated desire to encourage a sense of community and coming together. This doesn't mean that these cocktails can't be enjoyed solo, because, honestly, what's better (and more self-indulgently wonderful) than a restorative, peaceful moment away from it all, holding a glass filled with crushed ice and liquid joy? That's what I think a cocktail is, what it deserves to be—joy.

Having said all that, this is not a book about the apéritif. This is a book inspired by the culture of social interaction that the apéritif promotes, and I am hoping to honor its traditions while taking it to a new frontier. These are cocktails inspired by the Greats—I'm talking Daiquiris, Manhattans, and beyond—and take cues from the well-stocked fridges and back bars of Italian cafés. You may see white port take the place of bourbon in an Old-Fashioned-esque recipe or vermouth in place of tequila in a Margarita-like refresher. While aromatized wines (essentially herb-infused wines) and the like may be the leads in this story, full-proof spirits are not off-limits; you may just see them applied in a way you are not accustomed to. In my Kitty Cat Chronicles (page 98), you'll see a combination of Lillet Rouge and Bonal Gentiane-Quina, an apéritif, where you might expect to see bourbon. Perhaps you love something Negroni-inspired, then I'd direct you to Same Difference (page 140), where a generous pour of fino sherry holds up the bitterness of cacao nib–infused Campari. Although our gins, whiskeys, tequilas, and rums are accustomed to taking center stage with hefty two-ounce pours, you'll see them used in smaller measures as a tool to make their low-ABV friends shine.

There is something truly magical about lifting one's drink in unison with a group of friends or complete strangers to commemorate a moment in time with the simple gesture of clinking glasses. It symbolizes a coming together and a shared appreciation of values. The big "Cheers!" is often the punctuation mark to an inspired speech, the beginning of a celebration, or a somber reminder of unity in a time of grief. It's a practice that crosses borders and opens up roads to new adventures. Well, I'm

here to argue that what fills your glass should be as thoughtful as that going-away speech your best friend gave you, or the toast your mother made on your wedding day. What fills your glass should lift you up and move you as much as the toast itself. And I'm no life coach, but to me that means not just mindlessly slamming down one vodka soda after the other. To me—and again, I'm no life coach—that means lowering the proof of my drink. Whether it's low-proof or no-proof, an inspired combination of flavors can shift one's mental state. I've never had a desire to get drunk, and the handful of times I found myself room-spinning drunk, I had zero fun. The drinks in these pages are those that help you create lasting memories, and as Hallmark-y as that may sound, it's the ethos behind the entire book.

How to Use This Book

Geared to be equally useful to the novice and the professional, this book goes beyond just listing ingredients and aims to tell a complete story, from exploring the recipes' origins to breaking down the techniques best suited for each individual cocktail. With almost two decades of experience, I've been fortunate enough to have been able to pick the brains of some of the greats of the cocktail and food world and along the way have adapted those important lessons and techniques into tangible and approachable blueprints to cocktail making. And, while I am a true believer that all drink makers should first and foremost have a solid technical foundation, at the end of the day, what matters most is that the drink tastes delicious—and will taste that much better with the addition of a disco ball. Because if we can't add whimsy or a wink as an ingredient, then no amount of perfectly clear, chiseled ice will make the cocktail taste better.

The recipes are divided into five sections, each representing a certain mood or energy. For example, in Gulpable Thirst Quenchers (page 88), you'll find tart, juice-forward cocktails—think sours and collinses. The Slow Sippers (page 136) chapter, on the other hand, is all about elegant and, yes, playful low-ABV renditions of heady drinks like the Manhattan and the Sazerac. To make many of the recipes in this book, you'll need to put in some work, not just by shaking or stirring but by prepping various syrups and infusions (see page 250) and seeking out bottles that may not be on display at your local liquor store. I want to acknowledge your effort, as I know it's a commitment, but one that I hope you will find rewarding. Whether it's an obscure fortified wine or a syrup I've asked you to make from scratch, I've done my very best to utilize various specialty ingredients in multiple applications. In addition, each recipe chapter ends with a fun little section I like to call "Easy-Peasy One, Two, Three," drinks with a two-bottle pickup, which is just pro-speak for two different bottles, a garnish (get it—one, two, three?). These drinks, created with ease and versatility in mind, are always built in the glass and true to the style of the chapter. Some are as simple as a favorite highball, while others utilize a delicious infusion that deserves a second showcase.

And lastly, a quick but important note about *taste*. Taste is personal. It's subjective. You will love some of these ingredients and cocktail recipes, and you will absolutely not care for others. That's okay! We can't all be a French fry! And if you don't like French fries, then I'm afraid you won't like any of these recipes or ingredients because every single one of them is best paired with an order of French fries, preferably with a healthy coating of salt (and a side of mayonnaise, which I fully recognize may cause some controversy).

So, without further ado, let's dive in!

ORIGIN STORY:

A LITTLE
ABOUT ME

I GUESS ONE COULD SAY IT ALL GOES BACK TO THE WHITE WINE SPRITZ.

I grew up in a vibrant and diverse household. Both my parents are classical musicians. My Japanese-American mother is a concert pianist, while my Israeli father is a conductor. Though based in Germany, my childhood was spent traveling the world's opera houses and concert halls while making stops to spend weeks with family around the globe. As a family, we communicated in a mumble-jumble of languages and ate plates of hodgepodge food, or mishmash as we affectionately called our everyday stir-fry pasta with leftover turmeric chicken. Classical music filled our house at all times (I didn't discover pop music until I was ten years old—thanks, MTV), and my parents entertained guests often. My mother's dinner parties were legendary—friends and family (myself included) would beg her to cook her famous meals, elegant dishes like baked salmon with parsley sauce and perfectly crisped potatoes followed by a dessert spread of cheesecake, chocolate almond cake, red wine–poached pears, and whipped cream (yes, I said spread!). While cooking, my mother would have her hair in a loose, low bun, an apron cinching her waist just so, and on the kitchen counter was the somehow always half-full *gespritzte* glass of white wine (with way more bubbly water than wine, a ratio she still stands by today). I remember always thinking how glamorous and effortless my mother looked while prepping for her parties. My play kitchen soon churned out elaborate four-course meals in the style of my mother, and I couldn't wait to grow up and host real dinner parties of my own, *gespritzte* glass of white wine and all.

Many of my father's work trips were to Italy, most frequently Venice. The beautiful opera house Teatro La Fenice served as my playground. I spent rehearsals running up and down its hallways, hiding behind costume trunks and under grand pianos. Opening nights were a big deal, and my mother would put my sister and me in dresses she often sewed herself. After the premiere, the cast would gather at the local Chinese restaurant and celebrate. By the end of the meal, I always ended up with my head in my mother's lap, the tables strewn with tumblers filled with some sort of red liquid and an orange slice. Of course, I would later learn that this mysterious elixir was a Campari and Soda.

New Year's was spent at my grandmother's house (on my mother's side) in Berkeley, California, and celebrated the Japanese way with my grandmother hosting a *shogatsu* party, an impressive feast attended by family and friends. We'd spend days preparing all of the traditional dishes, such as kuromame (sweet black soy beans), gobo (burdock root), and of course platters of sushi and sashimi. Once guests arrived and the sake was warmed, I was always tasked with walking around and filling everyone's glasses.

I was eleven years old and living in Rome when my parents separated. Not knowing where to go next, my mother pulled out a map of the United States, then asked me to close my eyes and point at a state. My finger landed on Washington State, and so my mother and I packed up and moved to Seattle, not knowing anything about the city or anyone who lived there (my sister was on her own journey of self-discovery attending university in Massachusetts). That first year was difficult. While we'd never exactly fit in anywhere before, for the first time in my life I felt like I was living in a foreign land. But after some time, we started to settle in, we slowly made new friends, and soon my mother returned to the kitchen, her white wine spritz in one hand, her other sprinkling herbed salt on a fillet of salmon. We were back in a groove, gathered around our dinner table.

At eighteen, I moved to New York City to attend New York University as a theater major. The move also marked my first job in the hospitality industry. With a recommendation from my sister, who was a regular at the bar, I somehow found myself bartending in an Irish pub in the East Village. I had zero professional hospitality experience (wait, how do you know what table gets what food? Table numbers? Amazing!) and quickly learned that being a gracious host went a long way when I had no idea how to make the Cosmos my guests requested. Within a few short months, I was well versed in pouring a Guinness and could fumble my way through the round of Kamikaze shots my Saturday regulars ordered.

After working every front-of-house position imaginable in the service industry—coat check, cocktail waitress in six-inch heels, host—I landed a job as a server at a little restaurant in NoHo that would change my life. Sure, I eventually married the bartender there, but it was my career that took a big 180. I soon found myself bartending brunches, churning out Mimosas and Blue Woo's, an ungodly sweet mixture of blueberry schnapps and cranberry juice. Eventually, I became the assistant general manager. At that point, I was one year post-graduation from NYU, spending my days auditioning and my nights at the restaurant. I slowly started dreading my auditions and instead looked forward to a busy Friday-night service. Not long after, I parted ways with my talent agents and decided I wanted to do this restaurant and bar thing full-time. It was during this moment of recalibrating my life that I was offered my first real cocktail bartending gig. Ready for a change and for the chance to learn a new skill set, I jumped at the opportunity. In bars I'd worked in previously, the use of a jigger meant a nitpicky owner who forbade their staff to free-pour and look "cool" (and if we are being honest with ourselves, half the reason anyone wants to be a bartender is to look cool). In this setting, however, the jigger was a tool willingly used *by* the bartender to ensure balanced cocktail creation. Bar spoons weren't just for grabbing hard-to-reach olives out of a jar; they were used to stir cocktails, because apparently some drinks were stirred and some were shaken! I didn't know it at the time, but I was training with some of the best in the biz. My eyes were opened to a whole new world of bartending and spirits. I remember taking my first sip of a properly made Manhattan—stirred with fresh vermouth, rye whiskey, a dash of Angostura bitters and garnished with a crimson brandy-soaked cherry pierced by a bamboo cocktail pick. It felt like new taste buds sprang into action. That bottle of Campari, which had collected dust at all my other bar gigs, could be turned into Negronis. Fresh lime juice was mixed with sugar and rum to make the most delicious, frothy Daiquiri. Dry vermouth was an *actual* ingredient in a Martini, not some stale liquid that one seasoned a glass with, and sherry wasn't some warm, overly sweet cough syrup, as I had thought, but an incredibly varied and complex fortified wine. Also—fortified wine! A discovery that led me to this crazy journey of making low-proof cocktails.

I dove headfirst into studying classic cocktails and their structure (see page 83, Inspired by the Greats). I started visiting other bars and examined their menus with a fine-tooth comb. I tasted and tasted and tasted. My guests seemed as thrilled as I was! This wasn't just drinking for drinking's sake; this was an experience to relish, to savor and enjoy, and maybe most important, it was an experience I wanted to share with others.

BACHAN   SISTER   ME   MA

At the end of my shifts, while others slung back shots of overproof whiskey, all I craved was a refreshing, comforting drink—a glass filled with ice, a couple ounces of white wine, and a generous slug of bubbly seltzer. My mother's *Gespritzte* of my childhood. Often too embarrassed to drink this "old lady drink," I would give in and down half a shot of the whiskey.

Over the years that followed, I honed my skill behind many wonderful bars such as Maison Premiere and Mayahuel, until I partnered with my dear friends Alex Day and David Kaplan to open Nitecap in 2014. Though the bar itself was small, I always had big dreams for Nitecap. Yes, of course, the drinks had to be phenomenal, the menu design innovative, and the décor inviting. But my dream was far more than that. I envisioned Nitecap as a true home and refuge for its staff, a safe space that encouraged and celebrated collaboration, political discourse, and creativity.

Within a few weeks of opening I realized I needed something in the space to anchor those sentiments, and so a disco ball was hung. The disco ball was small in size and was connected to a remote control, allowing the staff to turn it on whenever they felt like the energy needed a little lift or to make a rendition of "Happy Birthday" that much more special. It was always, without fail, a unifying moment for everyone in the room—a shared moment of joy.

Nitecap also marked my first time in full control of a bar program, I wanted to make sure I paid homage to the drink that started it all for me—yup, the white wine spritz—and on our inaugural menu it took shape in an orange wine spritz made with bitter and bright Cocchi Americano Bianco, chamomile-infused blanc vermouth, tart verjus, and hard sparkling cider (Pinkies Out, page 90). Yes, a far departure from the traditional recipe, yet rooted in the easygoing structure and vibe of the classic. It was this drink that inspired me to spread the good word of low-ABV drinking.

What always drew me to low-ABV drinking, or as it's commonly known, the apéritif, is the social aspect of it. As my mother's dinner parties showed me, an apéritif is best enjoyed with a group of friends over lively conversation. It's romantic and charming, and it can extend a pleasant afternoon into a spontaneous dinner, then dessert and a nighttime stroll, and perhaps even a spin under a disco ball. The alcohol content is low, so you get a lovely little buzz but can remember everything the morning after.

So why all this backstory about growing up? I believe that taste and flavor are intensely personal and emotional. For me, everything in this book is tied to a memory, a feeling, or a place. Plus I'm a Cancer, and, yes, I'm highly emotional and read too deeply into everything, but my hope is that these recipes give you joy, make you dance, kiss longer, skinny-dip, truly relish that last bite of dessert, and refrigerate your vermouth.

The Politics of Disco

Let's talk about Disco. You'll notice that the imagery, colors, and mood of this book are a nod to the era of sequin bodysuits, light-up dance floors, and catchy beats. But what many people don't think about are the *politics* of disco. Disco was a celebration of self-expression and inclusion. It was a genre that celebrated Black pride, women's liberation, and civil rights, and that served as the anthem of the Stonewall uprising. It was a way to mentally escape economic inequalities following an era of social and political upheaval—the Vietnam War, race riots, the assassinations of JFK, Malcolm X, and Martin Luther King Jr. Disco was a direct response to the rise in puritanical politics that followed this period of justified unrest. It was a movement for those on the fringes of society. The dance floor served as a safe space, a platform of inclusion and open-mindedness. When I opened Nitecap, I was tired: tired of the rampant sexism in our industry, the abuse from so-called guests, and the whiteness of the cocktail landscape. I wanted Nitecap to be different, to *feel* different, and to have a unique voice in our community. There was a trend at speakeasy-type bars to post signage for rules of conduct, so at Nitecap we flipped that idea on its head and instead shared our manifesto of inclusion. An ode to the legacy of the disco dance floor, it included "We welcome and celebrate all ethnicities, all countries of origin, all religions, all genders" and was a popular item for souvenir thieves. While there was little space to dance (the bar was teeny-tiny), people often found creative ways to dance under the glimmer of our disco ball. Perhaps it is naive to think that in a huge, commanding city like New York, my little bar on the Lower East Side could have had any impact, but I sure hope it did, whether you were a guest punctuating a major moment with a cocktail or a staff member who hopefully had a positive work experience. So bring on the sparkles and the high-rise spandex pants, and also remember to celebrate comradery, togetherness, and differences, because that is what we do when we clink our glasses in a collective "Cheers!"

LOW-ABV ESSENTIALS:

ELEMENTS OF A TRULY WONDERFUL LOW-ALCOHOL DRINK

MY MANTRA WHEN CREATING NEW RECIPES IS "LOOK TO YOUR ELDERS!" AND BY THAT I MEAN LOOK BACK AT THE CLASSICS.

There is a reason certain cocktails have stood the test of time (hello, Old-Fashioned, I'm talkin' about you) and why we'd rather forget about others (Fuzzy Navel, anyone?). I think of each cocktail as falling within a certain family of cocktails. Each family has its matriarch, then the offspring. Basically, cocktails are one big happy boozy family tree. I've narrowed my tree to seven major branches: the Sour, the Daisy, the Highball, the Spritz, the Martini, the Old-Fashioned, and the Alexander. While some would argue that there are more, or fewer, categories, it's these I find most helpful when building cocktail templates. That's our key word, folks—*templates*. Even the Fuzzy Navel was built on a template; it was just executed without regard to balance. And balance is what differentiates a perfectly fine drinkable cocktail from an extraordinarily gulpable mindbender. But I don't mean "mindbender" as in getting so drunk you don't remember your own name. I'm talking about an absolutely fantastic cocktail that can transport you to a different realm, create a better mindset and a new invaluable memory. The following chapters cover the elements that need to be checked off for a cocktail to be successful.

Balance

Booze becomes a cocktail once it is mixed with other ingredients, and making sure that those ingredients sing in harmony with each other is the first step to cocktail nirvana. In many ways *balance* is a sort of catchall word for the following multiple flavor factors that must be considered.

SWEETNESS

Although many of us like to think that we don't like sweet cocktails, sweetness is a necessary component in a well-made cocktail. This doesn't mean, however, that all cocktails that employ a sweet player taste like a Mudslide (if you don't know what that is, it's a creamy concoction with a heavy dose of both Bailey's and Kahlúa, which can make your teeth hurt but is also admittedly devilishly delicious on occasion). Sweetness can come in many forms, such as a sugar-based syrup, a liqueur, or a generous pour of sweet vermouth à la the classic Manhattan. Sugar is also what I like to call an amplifier, meaning it has the ability to make flavors stand out and be the best version of themselves. A strawberry, for example, will taste more strawberry-y with a light sprinkling of sugar,

a banana more banana-y if you fry it up and caramelize all of its natural sugars. Here are some sweeteners that I like to use:

SIMPLE SYRUP: Equal parts white sugar and water, this mixture is neutral in flavor and is really just a carrier that supports the rest of the ingredients. Please note that I do not heat my simple syrup but rather only blend or whisk it to make sure it remains as neutral in flavor as possible.

CANE OR DEMERARA SYRUP: Two parts sugar to one part water, this mixture adds some nuanced caramel notes to a cocktail. I love demerara for its almost toffee-like flavor, which is why it's my go-to in an Old-Fashioned. Feel free to sub in turbinado sugar. You know that Sugar in The Raw box you can find at almost all grocery stores? While I'd say it has more molasses notes than cane or demerara, it makes for a solid understudy. To maintain their "uncooked" flavor, I don't heat these syrups either.

FLAVORED SUGAR SYRUPS: Using a neutral sugar base, I (and you!) can make everything from fresh raspberry syrup, cinnamon bark syrup, or even vanilla syrup using a high-quality extract (see pages 252 to 256 for recipes). For a more layered syrup, in terms of flavor, I'll use a darker sugar like demerara or even muscovado, which reminds me of biting into a dried date.

MOTHER NATURE'S CANDY: I like to think of ingredients like honey and agave syrup as beautiful sugar-wrapped gifts from our wondrous planet (and yes I know, regular old sugar comes from nature as well). These can dramatically vary in flavor and make for an excellent addition in cocktails.

JAMS AND PRESERVES: I often use these in addition to a neutral sugar syrup.

LIQUEURS: A liqueur is a spirit with the addition of flavors, such as fruits and herbs, and a healthy dose of sugar. Liqueurs vary in sweetness and intensity, and I usually use them in micro-doses, accompanied by a neutral sugar syrup.

ACIDITY

In some cases, I want to counterbalance sweetness with an acid. I like to think of the acidic element as a high note that brightens and enlivens a cocktail. It can take something from cloyingly sweet to tart and juicy. The combination of this magical sweet and acidic pairing has of course been grossly bastardized in the form of sour mixes, derived from some sort of powdery synthetic substance that eventually squirts out of a soda gun into your Margarita. Say no to pre-fab sour mix and instead welcome the following into your home:

FRESH CITRUS JUICES: Lemon and lime juices are the most widely used. Lemons are sharp in acidity and slightly sweet and usually pair best with aged spirits such as whiskeys and cognacs, as they act as sort of disruptors. Limes, while obviously tart, also have an inherent bitterness. They are most commonly paired with unaged spirits such as white rum or gin. Of course, this isn't a steadfast rule, as every cocktail is unique and free to express itself however it chooses. Oranges have an almost rounded sweetness, which is why I never use orange juice as an acidifier on its own. Grapefruit offers a bracing bitterness, which I'll usually balance out with another citrus. And then each citrus also has its varieties, from Meyer lemons, which possess a highly fragrant skin, to yuzu, which leaves your tongue tingling with delight, to mandarins and blood oranges.

VINEGARS: For an earthy, musky brightness, I love adding a bit of unfiltered apple cider vinegar. For a clean, drying effect, I'll reach for rice vinegar. The world of vinegars is huge and wondrous, and its vastness is something I don't think many of us contemplate. But I did all the contemplating and research for you, and the variety is unbelievable. Yeah, sure, balsamic is great, but have you ever tried rich, unctuous aged white balsamic vinegar? Coconut vinegar is pretty cool and makes for an excellent base in a shrub. Or mango vinegar, which is just as magical as it sounds? And that's just the start.

Texture

Through texture, we create a whole new level of sensory memory. How you remember a moment in time can be strongly impacted by how something literally feels to the senses—was the blanket scratchy or soft as a bunny; was the bathwater lukewarm or welcomingly hot? The same goes for mouthfeel, which is the tongue's way of discerning texture. Some drinks call for an airy, light texture that dances on the tongue; others should coat the mouth and linger with all of their velvety plush-ness.

Working with low-ABV spirits can present a number of challenges, including a loss of texture. Many low-ABV bottles are lighter in body, which often translate to a paper-thin texture. And while this lighter weight might be perfect for something like a traditional wine spritz, once you start adding citrus and a shaker into the equation, it can result in an unsatisfying drinking experience. Here are some ways I incorporate texture into my low-ABV recipes:

SYRUPS AND MOTHER NATURE'S CANDY: Sugar-based syrups and gooey (in the best way possible) things such as honey instantly add viscosity to a cocktail.

JAMS AND PRESERVES: Jarred fruit spread comes in handy once again! All the lovely pectin in jams helps create a beautiful, lush mouthfeel.

FULL-PROOF BOOZE: By this I mean alcohol that is 40 percent ABV or higher. I'll use it in small doses, just to give a cocktail that extra oomph factor.

Dilution

Dilution is a fancy way of saying "water," and water is a roundabout way of saying "ice." Without the addition of water, one is just drinking booze and mixers out of a fancy glass. You can achieve dilution via shaking or stirring (more on that, pages 48-51), and it will help you integrate all of the components of a drink into one silky/frothy sip of delights. Add too little water, and a cocktail can feel overwhelming; add too much, and flavors and texture start getting lost. Dilution can also be added by literally pouring water into a built drink, which is a technique I'll use when I'm batching cocktails that I'll chill in the freezer or fridge rather than shaking or stirring.

Temperature

One of the first things I always tell bartenders looking for advice on how to create cocktails is "Temperature is an ingredient!" I can't think of anything more disappointing than being served a Margarita in a gorgeous tumbler, garnished with a vibrant green lime wedge, only to discover upon the first sip that it is at room temperature. GAH. So, as simple as this may sound, make sure that a hot drink is hot and that a cold drink is cold (we'll touch on this again when we talk about technique, pages 48-51).

Presentation

This might seem superficial, but there's no denying that presentation dramatically affects how we perceive taste. I might even argue that presentation is the most important "ingredient." A glass of Champagne will automatically taste different when served in a red Solo cup, just as a Bud Light tastes different when sipped out of a crystal goblet. Ask yourself: would the drink benefit from a paper umbrella or a sprinkle of edible glitter? In my world, most drinks benefit from special touches in presentation. But don't forget that restraint can sometimes be the most impactful statement.

Smell

We must consider how the cocktail smells, as we quite literally taste with our noses. Something as simple as expressing a lemon peel over a cocktail has a dramatic effect on how our body responds to the drink. The fresh mint bouquet tucked neatly next to your straw is there so that you inhale all those cooling menthol notes upon your first sip (btw, this is me kindly asking all of you who immediately rip the mint out of your drinks to keep it in place). I always make sure to express some sort of citrus peel over an egg white cocktail because, truth be told, putting your nose into an egg white can feel like submerging all of your senses into the back of a musty fridge.

TOOLS AND TECHNIQUES:

SETTING YOURSELF UP FOR SUCCESS

SOME PEOPLE WILL SAY THAT COCKTAILS ARE JUST A LIST OF INGREDIENTS MIXED TOGETHER. I'M HERE TO ARGUE THAT POINT.

They will say that anyone who can follow a recipe can make a good drink. But a cocktail is more than the sum of its parts. It's a craft that requires patience, training, and constant refinement. We must commit to continually digest new knowledge and absorb different points of view. Combine this hunger for growth with precision and you'll find that the fruits of your cocktail labor taste that much better, not just to yourself, but also to those you share your creations with.

Use this chapter in the book as a glossary, as I'll be referring to one or more of these terms in each recipe. Refer to the Marketplace and Resources section (page 266) to help you find what you need.

How Good a Drink Tastes Goes Beyond Technique and Expensive Bar Gadgets.

One thing I always tell bartenders I'm training is that taste is highly influenced by environment. If you're sitting at a bar and the company you're keeping is fabulous, the playlist is on point, and the lighting makes your skin glow, you probably won't even notice if your Manhattan was shaken within an inch of its life and served in a lukewarm rocks glass, because you are so wrapped up in your joyful state of being. On the other hand, if your drink is made with perfectly chiseled clear ice and stirred in a crystal Japanese mixing glass but the company you keep is thoroughly mind-numbing and the music is a downer, no thoughtfully chilled, daintily etched Nick and Nora glass will save your taste buds from cocktail disappointment. All that being said, having charming friends isn't everything, and proper technique and tools do indeed make a difference. So, if you can have the perfect playlist, the perfect lighting, the perfect company, *and* the perfect cocktail, you've pretty much made it.

Tools of the Trade

BEHIND THE BAR

These are in alphabetical order, not in order of importance, as they are all important, thank you very much. Also please see my shopping suggestions for all of these goodies in Marketplace and Resources (page 266).

ATOMIZER: By this I mean a small bottle with a spray top. You can invest in a schmancy one or just get a small one-ounce glass bottle with a spray top. I use this for absinthe rinses or if I want to finish a cocktail off with some sort of flavored mist.

BAR SPOON: My go-to is a 30- to 35-centimeter, slightly weighted teardrop spoon. For best results, hold your spoon upward from the middle. I love the ones from Cocktail Kingdom but have also been known to use silly novelty spoons, which, as long as they have the same tightly wound spiral shape, do the trick.

FANCY BITTERS BOTTLES: These special bottles aren't just here for their looks, they also serve a practical purpose. Buy a bottle of bitters at the store and each dash will measure out differently as the volume inside the bottle changes. Fancy bitters bottles, on the other hand, have special dashers designed to make every dash exactly the same, allowing for consistency in your drink making. Urban Bar and Umami Mart make some of my faves.

FINE STRAINER: I use a simple cone-shaped fine strainer for two reasons: One, for any cocktail shaken and served up. Why? Because I'm not a fan of those little ice chips. I want my shaken Daiquiri to be light and frothy, and clunky ice chips interrupt that sensation. Secondly, I use it for any cocktail that has muddled fruit or herbs. Some people like seeing little pieces of mint floating in their drink. I do not. As herbs sit in the cocktail and macerate further, they tend to get bitter. Plus, that date you're on won't be so sexy when you have little pieces of basil stuck in your teeth. If I wanted a fruit salad in my cocktail, I would rather just eat a fruit salad. Of course, there are exceptions to the rule, and you'll see them pop up throughout the book. Cocktail Kingdom makes a great workhorse cone-shaped fine strainer, enabling the drink to get into your glass faster.

HAWTHORN STRAINER: A strainer made for using with shaker tins. This strainer has a metal spring that fits nice and snug into your tin and acts as a pretty good catchall for ice and any other solids such as muddled fruit. A good hawthorn strainer will have a little finger ledge, if you will, that aids you in pushing the lip of the strainer all the way over the edge of your tin, making it that much more effective in straining (I call this closing your gate). I love the Koriko Hawthorn strainer and the Buswell 4-Prong strainer, both available through Cocktail Kingdom. They feel sturdy and get the job done.

JIGGER: I recommend two types of jiggers: one that measures both ½ ounce and ¾ ounce, and another measuring 1 ounce and 2 ounces. Of course, a graduated jigger has all these measurements, often also including the ¼-ounce marker, in one compact jigger. I can't stress this enough: use your jigger! Making cocktails is like baking. Measure the baking soda wrong and your cake won't rise. Same goes for a cocktail. In fact, I implore you to make yourself a simple cocktail like a Sour and just change the proportion of your simple syrup by ¼ ounce in either direction. You will have an entirely different, and unbalanced, cocktail. That being said, also make sure you use your jigger correctly. If you are going to go through the trouble of using a tool, use it right. This means holding your jigger level and filling your jigger all the way to the correct denominations. Sounds simple and easy, but you'll be amazed how many people don't use their jiggers correctly.

JULEP STRAINER: This strainer is designed to be used with a mixing glass. Unlike the hawthorn strainer, a julep strainer has larger holes for the liquid to pass through, letting your cocktail pour out with less interruption—which is another step in helping the cocktail maintain its desired texture. However, I will add that for many of the larger-mouthed mixing glasses, I will use a hawthorn strainer in order to get a snug fit and avoid any rogue ice chips from plopping into the finished product.

KNIVES: I use two types of knives, a small paring knife and a large serrated one. The small is perfect for any detail work, such as slicing beautiful lemon or lime wedges, deseeding citrus, or cutting slim delicate cucumber disks. The larger serrated knife is for cutting citrus in half and slicing larger fruit such as grapefruits into crescents.

MICROPLANE: I use this to grate fresh citrus peel or dried spices such as nutmeg and cinnamon on top of cocktails.

MIXING GLASS: I'm a fan of a chilled, glass mixing glass—a simple weighted pint glass will do just fine. If you can get your hands on a Japanese-style mixing glass, fantastic. As the circumference of the glass is larger, you'll automatically have more surface space for your cocktail while you stir. Umami Mart has some beautiful simple options, while Urban Bar makes some great large-format mixing glasses.

MUDDLER: I recommend a sturdy, weighted muddler with a flat top. Muddling should really just be a simple couple of taps to slightly break up whatever fruit or herb the recipe calls for. There is a trend to overmuddle things and beat the juicy fruit or delicate herb to a pulp—do not subscribe to this trend! Muddling should be a gentle yet direct action. The ice in your shaker will also do some of the work for you when you shake.

PEELER: You'll need a peeler for making citrus twists and ribbons of all kinds. Using a peeler can be risky business and should be practiced and never done in a rush. Wanna hear about the time I was behind the bar and sliced my fingertip off while making a lemon twist at 8 p.m. on a Saturday night when we were down one bartender?! Your peeler should be sharp and replaced when it becomes dull. While you want to handle the peeler with a firm grip, avoid pushing it down into citrus peels, as your goal when making a citrus peel is to leave behind most of the white pith. My favorite peelers are the super-cheap Y-shaped ones that you can buy at pretty much any grocery store. No need to buy something extravagant here.

SHAKER SET: In my humble opinion, the best shaker set is metal on metal (not metal on glass). The perfect combination is a 28-ounce weighted shaker with an 18-ounce weighted shaker. I'm a fan of Koriko shaker sets.

TEASPOON SET: The two spoons you'll be called upon to use are ½ teaspoon and 1 teaspoon. I remove the rest of the spoons and save them in my kitchen drawer for other uses.

BEHIND THE SCENES

BLENDER: Sure, blenders are a source of cocktail joy, because after all, what's better than a slushy? But I also use a blender to mix up syrups and make nut milks. It's an investment, but nothing beats a Vitamix.

CITRUS JUICER: All juices (well, almost all) are fresh squeezed. A simple handheld juicer will do just fine. If you're looking to upgrade, you can find all sorts of motorized citrus presses that will help you with efficiency and ultimate extraction. For high-volume juicing, or if you want to flex, Sunkist makes the most durable and effective juicer.

CHINOIS: A large, cone-shaped fine-mesh sieve is great for straining infusions or syrups with large particles.

EXTRACTOR: Anything fibrous or noncitrus will need to be juiced in an extractor. I'm talking fresh ginger, celery, beets, carrots, and apples. Having one of these in your kitchen arsenal is a game changer when it comes to cocktail making because you are able to use ingredients in a way that lets them express themselves in their truest form. Champion makes an incredibly sturdy model, perfect for stubborn ingredients like ginger, that I use at all of my bar projects. At home, I have a great Breville one, which on occasion even inspires me to make green juices.

GRAM SCALE AND MICROGRAM SCALE: Many of my syrup or infusion recipes call for you to weigh ingredients rather than measure by volume, as weight is more reliable than volume.

IMMERSION CIRCULATOR OR SOUS VIDE MACHINE: This piece of equipment is designed to cook ingredients in a temperature-controlled water bath while *sous vide* (under vacuum). I'll go into this more in the Syrups and Infusions chapter (page 250).

NUT BAG OR SUPERBAG: These reusable, hand-washable bags are perfect for straining syrups, infusions, fresh juices, and the nut milk used to make homemade orgeats. I like to keep a few around and assign different job categories to each. For example, I have one that I use solely for fat washes, one for fruit, and another for dry ingredients. They have a tight weave that allows only what you want to come through. You can find all sorts of different-sized superbags at Modernist Pantry.

The Kit: It's composed of three parts—a black Sharpie, a roll of masking tape, and a pair of scissors. At Nitecap, they were kept together in a little box because they should never be separated! Use this kit to label and date all of your homemade syrups, juices, and infusions. There is no ripping of masking tape, people! It is to be neatly cut with the scissors. And while we are here, always make sure to face your labels outward and to rotate everything according to usage date.

Glassware

In the most perfect of worlds, all glassware, save the julep tin and toddy mug, should be chilled before being filled with a cocktail. Many cocktail bars, including Nitecap, have precious real estate taken up by freezers specifically designated for keeping glassware cold, because it's that important. If you can't dedicate to chilling everything (but promise you'll try, okay?), please make sure at least to *always* chill your coupe and Nick and Nora glasses.

COUPE

Size: 6 to 7 ounces
I like to use a coupe glass for all my cocktails shaken and served up. The larger surface area allows that frothy layer of heaven to settle just right. Since cocktails served in a coupe aren't served over ice (at least not

in my cocktail world), I always demand the glass be chilled before use to ensure the ideal temperature for your lively cocktail— holding the stem of course helps the drink stay cold for as long as possible, too.

A QUICK NOTE ABOUT THE SIZE OF YOUR GLASS: I'm not a fan of having the wash line* of my drink right up to the tippity top of my glass. As someone who has carried a lot of cocktails on trays in their lifetime, that sinking feeling when you walk up to the service bar and see six cocktails in dainty little glasses filled to the brim is enough to make you wonder why you are being set up for failure and want to quit your job on the spot. Additionally, as the person drinking the cocktail, I don't want to have to take my first sip by dipping my face into the glass for fear of spilling it all over my lap. So, in conclusion, we love a stemmed, delicate coupe glass that looks full but isn't an accident waiting to happen.

*Bar lingo: The wash line is the place the drink hits in relation to the glass.

DOUBLE ROCKS

Size: 12 to 14 ounces

This is my favorite glass for anything shaken or stirred, served on the rocks, and not topped with any sort of bubble. We're talking Margaritas and Negronis. If the drink isn't served over crushed ice, I always use a large-format ice block for this glass. It just feels like a sturdy combination in my hands. If you are wondering whether to straw or not-straw, my vote falls very confidently in the not-straw zone, unless it's served over crushed ice, as the shape of this glass lends itself perfectly to some good old-fashioned mouth-to-mouth contact, allowing the liquid to effortlessly flow to make the perfect-sized sip.

FESTIVE

Size: 16 ounces

This is your party-on-crushed-ice-transport-yourself-to-your-happy-place glass! This category is a total wild card, so as long as it fits the size requirements, go bananas. For some drinks that fall into this category, I prefer a sleek footed tulip glass, just to add a little elegance to my completely off-the-wall coconut bonanza. For others, I want to go all out—neon, pink, iridescent, cat-shaped—go for it! Whimsy and fantasy are your best friends here.

YOU MIGHT BE WONDERING . . . isn't Natasha just describing a tiki glass?! I suppose that in the modern cocktail lexicon, these sorts of glasses are by default called tiki glasses. But "tiki," as both a term and a bar culture, is something we should all further examine and question. I was always disturbed by the tiki world's hypersexualization and exotification of brown-skinned and Asian women, and I'll be the first to admit that up until quite recently, I very willingly turned a blind eye to tiki culture's dark and exploitative ways. What could possibly be harmful about luau-themed parties and extravagantly garnished tropical rum cocktails? The first thing to point out is that a tiki is a deified ancestor throughout Polynesian culture. Somewhere along the way, someone decided it was acceptable to use these sacred images in their fantasy island narrative. Tiki bar culture is a muddled narrative at best. It borrows elements of a fabricated and idyllic lifestyle, when in fact there is a long, violent history of colonialism that persists today throughout the Pacific Islands. Plainly put, "traditional" tiki mugs and the drinking culture that accompanies them can only be defined as a whitewashing of history and current ongoing struggles. This tiny paragraph doesn't give this subject the space or weight it rightly deserves, but hopefully it ignites the little revolutionary spark in you to do more research on your own.

FIZZ

Size: 8 ounces

I like to think of these as mini-highball glasses. They are designed for luscious egg white fizzes or whole egg flips that are not served over ice.

HIGHBALL

Size: 10 to 12 ounces

I mostly use highball glasses for anything that is elongated with bubbly soda and served over ice, such as a Gin and Tonic or Tom Collins. I'm pro-straw as well. Obviously, no plastic. I go for reusable metal ones. If looking for a good disposable option, I'm a fan of hay straws and avocado pit straws. (Yup! Those truly exist and don't get soggy.) Why the straw? These are the sorts of drinks you want to be able to take nice long sips from, but taking a sip directly from the glass means being attacked by ice cubes.

JULEP TIN

Size: 14 ounces

Though a double rocks glass will often do just fine, certain cocktails simply taste better when served from a gorgeous and shiny julep tin! The material ensures that your crushed ice stays cold longer, giving your drink longevity.

MUG

Size: 12 to 14 ounces

For hot drinks I like to use a mug with a handle. Depending on my mood, I want something either ceramic and sturdy that screams, "Let's sit around a fire pit," or, if I'm feeling more festive, something glass. Either way, make sure to preheat your mugs before use so your drink stays toasty and warming.

NICK AND NORA

Size: 5 to 6 ounces

I use a Nick and Nora glass for all my stirred-up cocktails like a 50/50 or for shaken cocktails that measure out on the smaller side, such as a Last Word, while still allowing for a little space up top. My motto when it comes to filling your glass: You have to be able to dance and/or gesture passionately and not spill the contents of your glass. As with a coupe, a cocktail in a Nick and Nora glass will not be served over ice, so make sure to chill it before use. In a perfect scenario, this glass is delicate, maybe even dainty, and very pretty and makes what you're drinking feel special.

SINGLE ROCKS

Size: 10 to 12 ounces

Got to be honest, I'm not a huge single rocks glass kind of girl. Many people drink their neat spirits in a single rocks glass, but I always prefer a cute stemmed mini glass, as I don't love the feel of a chunky, room-temperature hunk of glass in my hands. I do, however, understand that this is the way most of the world enjoys their neat spirits, so there must be good reason behind its popularity. What I do love a single rocks glass for is a cocktail like a Sazerac, however, it must *without exception* be chilled first!

SNIFTER

Size: 10 to 12 ounces

I think the word *snifter* makes people immediately think of some sort of exclusive high-society meeting in a private wine cave. And while I'm sure many cufflink-wearing hands grip this glass on the regular, let's make this a glassware choice for all people (btw, I love cufflinks, so I'm not bashing them). Essentially just an exaggerated wineglass, a snifter is designed to help you experience all the aromatics a liquid has to offer. It's a wonderful way to taste spirits on their own or to give your Sazerac drinking experience a glow-up. And to that I enthusiastically say yes, please!

V-MARTINI

Size: 5 to 6 ounces

While I serve most of my up stirred drinks in a Nick and Nora, some drinks are begging to be served in a V-Martini glass, and, honestly, a V-Martini glass looks really good with a sequined jumpsuit.

WINEGLASS

Size: 12 to 14 ounces

Before we even start debating, a wineglass—for the purpose of this book—should always be stemmed. Look, I'm not above drinking wine in a tumbler à la cute Italian cafés, but in this setting, I'm choosing glassware very intentionally, and in this case, I stand behind a stem. While my general preference for any glass rim is thin and delicate, I find it extra important for a wineglass. Imagine yourself sipping, let's say, our good friend the Aperol Spritz. In scenario number one, you are holding a chunky monster of a goblet. You take a sip and are met with a medieval wall of glass. In scenario number two, you are holding a lovely all-purpose wineglass with a delicate rim. You take a sip and aren't distracted by an intruder in your mouth, but instead are met by a delightful fizz.

Techniques

SHAKEN VERSUS STIRRED

Before we dive into exploring technique, it's important to touch on what exactly differentiates a shaken from a stirred cocktail. The general rule of thumb (and you'll discover that in the cocktail world, not all rules are universal) is that a drink containing any opaque ingredients, by which I mean juice, egg, or cream, should be shaken. As these ingredients lean on the more viscous side of the spectrum, they need to be shaken with vigor and effort in order to be properly integrated into the cocktail. A stirred cocktail, on the other hand, will be made up mostly of spirits with modifiers such as vermouth, bitters, and sugar-based syrups. Why this rule? It all comes down to texture. Shaking and stirring can both accomplish dilution and chilling, but shaking also aerates the ingredients, making them frothy and lively, while stirring helps maintain a smooth and silky mouthfeel. Either technique can bring a list of ingredients to life.

SHAKEN

Our goal when shaking a cocktail is to awaken and incorporate all of its components. Nothing sounds more unappealing than flaccid lime juice or a chunky gulp of egg whites. And, yes, I just did my best to make that sound as unappealing as possible. If I could have added the word *moist* to the mix, I would have. In my attempt to disgust you, I'm hoping you'll feel inspired to breathe life into your shaken concoctions. It will require a proper stance, muscle, and stamina.

A quick note on my shaking technique: As bartenders, it is not uncommon to clock a nine- or ten-hour shift. That's nine or ten hours on your feet, interacting with guests, constructively communicating with the rest of your team, trying to execute orders efficiently, all the while trying to gracefully navigate your own emotions and fatigue. The shake I've developed for myself is a direct response to my overworked body—years of physically draining work had begun to take its toll on my muscles and bones. It can feel silly to examine a shake like this; after all, we are just making cocktails, not performing brain surgery. However, your health and the liveliness of your cocktails are truly important to me. It took time and many other unsuccessful shake techniques to land on this one. If you've never picked up a cocktail shaker in your life, this may be a good place to start, and you can adapt it however you feel fit. If you're a seasoned pro and are currently on your couch recovering from a grueling solo Monday-night shift that was unexpectedly busy and your back is spasming, maybe this can be a stepping-stone to a stronger, less achy you. I find that this shake is easy on my shoulders and back, that I can sustain the same energy and gusto from the first cocktail I make to the last cocktail I make, all the while creating delicious and gorgeous drinks for my guests to enjoy.

Once my cocktail is assembled in my small shaker tin, I add my shaking-ice, seal the shaker, firmly grab it, and turn sideways away from my guest. I do this so that I can shake with full intensity without having to worry that my shaker might explode on my guest, and it's true, all bartenders, myself included, have horror stories about flying shaker tins.

My left hand has a firm grip on the larger bottom tin while my right hand is extended over both the top of the small tin with my thumb and the connection point of the two tins with my middle and ring fingers.

I assume my stance. It's the same every time: right foot slightly in front of my left foot. If you're a dancer, think of it as a very crude fifth position with terrible turnout. I bring my arms up, elbows bent and out, shaker still in hands, to the middle of my chest bone.

Make a few gentle shakes to start. I like to think of these initial few moves as an introduction for the liquid and the ice to calm the shock of warm ingredients hitting freezing cubes.

Then I shake. My shake moves in oval waves. Just like the waves in an ocean, although soothing to listen to and watch,

each movement is filled with intention, force, power, and strength. The ice in my shaker is moving in such a way that its corners are becoming rounded, not smashed.

Length of shake depends on what kind of cocktail I am making (more on this later).

Once I sense that the cocktail is ready, I immediately strain the drink into its glass using a hawthorn strainer, making sure to do so in a swift manner, as the ice in my tin is now fully compromised and deteriorating at a steady pace.

Each "shaken" drink recipe in this book will call for one or more of these shakes:

Shake

Our standard shake, lasting about 20 to 25 seconds with either a full scoop of cubed ice or a combination of one large ice block and two ice cubes. If the cocktail is served up (no ice), I tend to veer toward the 25-second mark. Conversely, if it's served over ice, veer toward the 20-second mark.

Short Shake

Often for cocktails served over crushed ice, lands in the 10- to 15-second mark with a full scoop of cubed ice. It should involve the same amount of physical effort as a regular shake.

Whip

For drinks in need of a quick chill and minor dilution, this shake means adding 3 to 5 pebble ice cubes to the drink and whipping the mixture until the ice has dissolved. I then dump the contents of my shaker into the glass.

Pre-shake

Often referred to as a dry shake, the pre-shake is to ensure that ingredients such as egg whites and cream are properly incorporated, emulsified, and aerated. A dry shake is a swift and efficient shake sans ice lasting between 10 and 15 seconds. For my pre-shake, I don't assume my regular oval shake stance and instead make this much more of a direct up-and-down motion to help ingredients that don't always want to be together to stay together, for example, citrus and egg white. A pre-shake is always followed by a shake with ice.

STIRRED

Our goal when stirring a cocktail is to create a smooth texture by adding dilution and reaching the ideal temperature without agitating the ingredients too much. I like to make sure that my mixing glass is chilled before I use it, ensuring that my cocktail reaches ultimate chilldom. Since the mixing glass is cold, it also means the ice I use to dilute the drink will stay colder longer. Additionally, to reach ideal dilution, using a chilled mixing glass will translate into needing to stir for a longer period of time than if I was using a room-temperature glass. For cocktails served up or ones that have more viscous ingredients, I will first hand-crack a few ice cubes into the built cocktail before adding the remaining whole cubes, to give the liquid more surface area to do its thing on, speeding the process up a bit.

Once my cocktail is assembled in the chilled mixing glass, I'll add the cubed ice, making sure that all the liquid is in direct contact with ice. For me this is filling the mixing glass a little over three-quarters of the way with ice.

Next, I'll insert my bar spoon, making sure it hits the bottom of the mixing glass. If my work surface is slippery or if the glass feels unstable in any way, I'll secure the mixing glass with my nondominant hand by making an L shape with my thumb and index finger and holding the mixing vessel at its base, that is, the lowest possible part of the mixing glass. Why? Because our hands are conductors of heat, and if we've just gone through the trouble of chilling the mixing glass, we are effectively undoing that step by holding the mixing glass in the warm palm of our hand.

With my dominant hand, I'll begin to stir. The motion is almost entirely in my fingers and can be likened to pulling and pushing the bar spoon back and forth. Not using my wrist and arm lets me create an even and effortless path, closely following

the circumference of the mixing glass and using it as my road.

Once I've reached my desired temperature and dilution, I'll add a few fresh ice cubes to my mixing glass. The main reason I do this is so that my cocktail gets one last extra chill through some fresh ice. The second reason is to make sure I can stabilize my julep strainer in such a way that little ice chips don't find a way to escape from the mixing glass into my finished product.

And lastly, it's important to acknowledge once again that we are in a race against time, so I swiftly pour my drink into its assigned glassware.

Built

These cocktails are quite literally assembled in the vessel they will be served in. These are drinks that don't require that initial burst of dilution and really just need to be chilled and given a little stir to incorporate everything together seamlessly, for example, a Whiskey Highball, a Vodka Soda, or, in our buzzy little world, a Vermouth and Tonic. For simple one-and-ones like these, I add ice to my glass and then build the ingredients over the ice, thereby chilling it, and once it's built I give it a couple of gentle stirs. If I'm building something a little more complex, like one of my wine spritz variations, I take a few extra steps:

- **Hand-crack three cubed ice cubes into the glass. This will dilute the ingredients just the right amount while also chilling things faster because you've created more surface space.**

- **Measure out all the nonbubbly ingredients and build them over the cracked ice.**

- **Fill the remainder of the glass with whole ice cubes.**

- **If recipe calls for bubbles, add those now.**

- **Stir everything together for 10 seconds and serve.**

BONUS POINTS: I'd been bartending for years when I walked into a training session for a new job at a place that shall remain unnamed because it ended up being a total dumpster-fire situation. That experience changed my life forever, because it was there that I formed a bond with Alex Day and David Kaplan, who would become my future partners at Nitecap. Alex and David were consulting on the property and were leading an intense two-week training for the bar staff. Here's how you jigger correctly. Here's how you pour correctly, etc., etc., and then BAM—and now you're going to learn to do everything again but with your other hand! To say I was resistant to becoming an ambidextrous bartender would be the understatement of the century. But reluctantly, and with seemingly insurmountable frustration, I followed along until, by the end of the training sessions, I was as comfortable bartending with my nondominant hand as I was with my dominant hand. I learned quickly that being ambidextrous behind the bar meant that I could literally stand in the same spot behind my well for most of the night, and instead of rotating my body to reach things, I could just extend my arms in either direction and grab things swiftly and efficiently. More important, I noticed an immediate shift in my body. Years of reaching over myself had put a serious strain on my back, and this new technique helped ground me and let my body move with ease for hours during a busy shift behind the service station. My advice to you: Learn everything you do with your dominant hand, and mirror your motions and placement of your ruling side with your nondominant hand and side. And now you, too, can become a ninja-octopus bartender.

PRO TIP: Taste, taste, taste! Make sure you are taste-testing your creations as you work. There's no better way to see if your Martini is at its perfect place than by quickly dipping in a straw (reusable, of course!) and checking its dilution and temperature.

THE PANTRY:

ESSENTIAL INGREDIENTS TO LOVE AND EMBRACE

FOR THE HOME COOK THERE IS ALWAYS THAT ESSENTIAL LIST OF MUST-HAVES AND THE SAME IS TRUE FOR THE HOME BARTENDER.

A well-stocked pantry ensures dinner can be prepared on the fly—the olive oil, salt, that can of whole peeled tomatoes, rice, beans. You catch my drift. Well, the idea of a pantry is just as crucial to the home bar. Have a curated list of ingredients to keep on hand, pop in a novelty item every now and then, and you can create a Rolodex of cocktails that are exciting, fresh, and fun. For me, that's what making and drinking cocktails is really about—an expression of playfulness and creativity, and the privilege of experiencing a new point of view. To discern what we need for our pantry, or in pro terminology, our back bar, we need to understand the vast world of ingredients available to us. And there are many, ranging from your true and tested friends vermouth and Lillet to the bottle of umeshu or Pineau des Charantes that you have no idea how to incorporate into a drink. Our ingredients cover a vast range of flavor profiles and span the globe. And with that I will add that many of the spirits that land on our liquor shelves have direct historical ties to oppression. Many also carry with them detrimental environmental implications and inhumane labor practices. Recognizing these realities, and acknowledging the complicated histories attached to what's in your glass, is a big step forward. I will always encourage you to seek out bottles that make transparency a priority.

This section is Spirits 101, where we will barely scratch the surface. My hope is that this foundation tickles your hunger for knowledge and that you somehow find yourself in your kitchen at the end of a long day lining up three different dry vermouths to compare and contrast them and how they can be applied in different scenarios. There's also on overwhelming amount of STUFF out there, so I'll make sure to mention a few of my faves along the way.

Note: If we actually want to get to the part where we start making delicious cocktails, it would be absolutely impossible to delve into each of these ingredient categories in great detail. So I'm going to paint you a general picture. Understanding how each ingredient is made will give you a greater appreciation for what's in your glass. I find that we often forget that every drop of liquid in every bottle is made by an actual living, breathing human being with their own very capable hands. There is a sort of transference that happens between the maker and their product, which allows for nuance and variety. Each distiller, winemaker, or brewer is simply trying to communicate something through their liquid to you, the drinker. And lest you forget, water has memory and can transform, so we are in essence drinking someone's life story. How fortunate are we?!

The Lingo

So, what exactly is an apéritif? Italy seems to have been the birthplace of this style of drinking and of the *aperitivo*. The word itself is derived from the Latin word *apiere*, "to open," signaling a culture of drinking that is accompanied by food, as the herb-ladened vermouth or spirit was meant to help enliven the taste buds and also calm the stomach. Italy, of course, is synonymous with Campari, a distinctively bitter red liqueur often mixed with a splash of seltzer and served as soon as the clock strikes 6 p.m. The piazzas quickly fill with groups of friends ready to snack on focaccia and salty cheese, all the while sipping Campari or Cinzano over ice. The almost cultlike appreciation of this sacred time is so ingrained in daily life that bars and cafés often serve the small bites accompanying the drink at no extra charge. If I'm currently describing heaven to you, then we are on the same page. You'll find similar scenes in France, Spain, and Germany. Europeans, however, weren't the only ones to think of pairing the end of daylight with some light imbibing and friends—another reminder that history isn't often told in complete stories. In Japan you'll find people sipping on sake while eating light appetizers, or *izakaya*, to start their evening. In Mexico you'll find a variety of different regional low-ABV brews, such as *tejuino*, which is made from a fermented mixture of masa and lime juice and is sipped during the day to accompany street-vendor snacks. Both of these, along with many other countries' traditions, are just as compatible within the framework of the European-conceived idea of apéritif hour. All across the globe, the magic hour that signals the transition between work and leisure, that celebrates the accomplishments of a day and the promise of a fun-filled night ahead, all accompanied by a bite and engrossing conversation, is the very essence of the apéritif, and it should indeed be for everyone.

WHAT IS AN AROMATIZED WINE? A wine that has been flavored with a variety of herbs, fruits, and spices that is often fortified.

WELL, WHAT DOES IT MEAN TO FORTIFY A WINE? To fortify a wine means adding a small amount of distilled spirit, thereby bringing its alcohol content up a few degrees. This process helps stabilize the wine and makes sure you can enjoy it longer.

WHAT IS THE DIFFERENCE BETWEEN LIQUOR AND A LIQUEUR? Liquor is very simply a distilled spirit. A liqueur is a liquor or wine that has been flavored and sweetened.

The Stars of the Show

It's hard to even quantify how many low-ABV spirits exist. I have tasted a lot, like *a lot*, of them and am painfully aware that I wasn't able to include them all here. This book and these recipes are simply a reflection of my current point of view, and I will hopefully shine a welcoming light on many of these underused bottles. The goal is to have you scouring your local liquor store or wine shop for some of these gems. Many quality fortified wines are amazingly affordable, so even though there are those unbelievably delicious bottles of $150 Pineau des Charantes, you won't see me call for them in any of my recipes. So say "hello!" to two full ounces of vermouth in your next sour.

WINE- AND FRUIT-BASED

APÉRITIF WINE

An aromatized and fortified wine, sometimes bitter, infused with barks, herbs, spices, and often chinchona bark.

Chinchona bark is what really defines the majority of this category. So, first off, what is chinchona? It's the bittering agent in tonic water also known as quinine. It's a flavor that really gets those taste buds working and causes you to salivate. Chinchona bark has been used for medicinal purposes for centuries, most notably to help cure malaria, although it was already widely used in South America before European colonization. Other apéritif wines are flavored with gentian root, which has a similar flavor profile but is slightly more bitter, gritty, and earthy.

Some of My Faves

- **Bonal Gentiane-Quina:** Made by infusing a mixture of herbs and barks from the Chartreuse Mountains, this namesake apéritif wine is surprisingly light in body with notes of just-picked wild raspberries.

- **Lillet Blanc:** A gorgeous, fragrant wine that feels like you are lying in a bed of orange blossoms while being fed vanilla pudding.

- **Cocchi Americano Rosa:** Bright and bitter grapefruit peel meets rose petals and a hint of ginger.

- **Byrrh Grand Quinquina:** Its deep, almost jamlike texture will make you wish you could spread this on toast.

MADEIRA

A fortified wine from the Portuguese island of Madeira uniquely made by repeatedly heating and cooling the wine.

This technique was discovered through pure happenstance when, during the 1600s and 1700s, barrels of wine were being shipped through the tropics and encountering various climates and temperatures. Nowadays, madeira makers use two methods to heat the wine. One way is called *canteiro*, requiring barrels to be aged slowly by sitting either in the sun or in warm, temperature-controlled rooms. The other is via *estufagem*, in which the wine is quickly heated in tanks over a period of three months. The wine also comes in different classifications, from affordable table wine versions often used in cooking, to ultra-luxe and rare bottles that most definitely should be sipped slowly, eyes closed, while wearing a silk robe.

Some of My Faves

- **H&H Rainwater 3-Year Madeira:** My go-to for mixing into cocktails, it's dry, nutty, and über-versatile.

PORT

A Portuguese fortified wine made with distilled grape spirit from the Douro Valley, which is then aged in oak barrels.

Port comes in three styles: white, pink, and, most commonly, red. Let's talk about red first. Its two classifications are Tawny and Ruby, the latter spending less time in oak barrels. To me, red port screams rich, red berries, plums, subtle notes of luxurious vanilla, and fragrant burnt cinnamon, and even in its sweetest iteration it is quite dry. White port, made from white grapes, is surprisingly rich in flavor. It makes me think of overripe peaches and apricots, toasted almonds, and caramelized citrus peels. Pink, or rosé, port feels like the teenage offspring of white and red. It is much more playful and doesn't take itself too seriously. It is, however, just as refined and boasts earthy raspberries and tart cranberries in its flavor profile.

Some of My Faves

- **Sandeman Fine Tawny Port:** Everything you want from a port—tons of tart cherry, vanilla, and jammy fig. It mixes into cocktails with ease.

- **Quinta do Infantado, White Port, NV:** This off-dry bottle mixes flawlessly into cocktails and is the perfect addition to a simple highball. Super nutty with a bright fresh lemony finish, this port is also made from organically farmed grapes. I love to sip on this with a slice of lemon.

SHERRY

In short (although truthfully there is no short way to describe sherry), a fortified wine made from white wine from Andalusia, Spain.

There is SO MUCH TO SAY about sherry, and if you are familiar with any of my cocktail recipes, you'll know that I sneak sherry into about 99.9 percent of my drinks. And I say "sneak" because sherry is misunderstood by a lot of people, but I am here to tell you that it is glorious and you should start drinking it immediately. There are many types of sherry, and they range from bone dry (like, drier than any dry white wine you've ever had) to almost syrupy and deliciously sweet. All are aged in oak casks, but some are aged biologically while others are aged oxidatively in a solera system, which is a highly involved process of blending wines of different ages in barrels. The types of sherry are Fino, Manzanilla, Amontillado, Oloroso, Palo Cortado, Moscatel, Pedro Ximénez, Dry Sack, and East India. The last two also fall into a category known as "cream sherries," which do not in fact contain cream, but rather are multiple styles of sherry blended together.

And to make things even more complicated, there are some sherries, like amontillado, that dip their toes in both styles of aging.

Some of My Faves

- **Lustau Los Arcos Amontillado Sherry:** I use this stuff like ketchup! It's dry, it's nutty, and it's super versatile. It's a great way to add depth to a cocktail and also simply yummy sipped chilled and neat to accompany food.

- **La Gitana Manzanilla:** This beautiful beverage is full of minerality and delicate notes of dried chamomile.

- **González Byass Pedro Ximénez:** This is like the best dessert in a bottle. Bursting with caramelized and overripe fruit notes, it's a real treat.

VERMOUTH

An aromatized and fortified wine that has been infused with various herbs, barks, and spices.

Often thought of as a supporting character in a Manhattan or Martini, in this little low-ABV universe, she is the North Star. Vermouth starts out as wine, is then fortified to between 16 and 18 percent alcohol, and finally is steeped with a proprietary mix of seasonings. Though vermouth has its roots in Italy and France, it's now being made all over the world, with some incredible makers in Spain and the US. There are four types of vermouth: sweet (rouge, rosso, or red), dry, white (blanc or bianco), and pink (rosé). Sweet vermouth is dark in color and often has richer baking-spice notes to it. Think vanilla, caramelized orange peel, cinnamon. Dry vermouth is, most often, clear in color and has more herbal, sometimes floral notes. Think tarragon, lemon peel, grass. White vermouth will also be clearish in color and in taste a hybrid of sweet and dry; it often reminds me of a bouquet of flowers picked in the wild. Think chamomile, elderflower, sage. And there is also pink vermouth, which can be delightful. Slightly fruitier, think tart strawberries complemented by earthy cardamom and lemon peel.

Some of My Faves

- **Carpano Antica Sweet Vermouth:** This sweet (rouge/rosso/red) vermouth is for when you want to go full-on rich, silky, and voluptuous. There is nothing quite like this gorgeous friend which many consider the benchmark of Italian sweet vermouths.

- **Dolin Dry Vermouth:** This classic dry French vermouth is the first bottle I always reach for when I want something reliable and delicate.

- **Dolin Blanc Vermouth:** My go-to for a white (blanc/bianco) vermouth. It tastes like dancing through the crisp clear air in the Alps, as if you were Julie Andrews.

- **Lustau Rosé Vermut:** I have a huge blush-worthy crush on his pink (rosé) vermouth with its hints of vanilla, berries, and anise—it truly gives me butterflies.

MISTELLE

An apéritif wine made by fortifying unfermented juice. Made in multiple distinctive ways according to region. Here they are broken down:

Floc de Gascone
An apéritif wine made by combing and aging a mixture of grape juice with Armagnac.

Maybe my favorite mistelle to drink, topped with a splash of seltzer. It comes in red, white, and pink varieties. I mean this in the absolute best way possible, but it reminds me a lot of Arizona Green Tea, you know, the one in the big green can. Bursting with notes of jasmine and honey, it's a true delight and adds a wonderful surprise to cocktails.

Macvin du Jura
An apéritif wine made by combining and aging a mixture of grape juice and marc, which is brandy made from grape pomace.

Made in three styles—white, rosé, and red—Macvin du Jura is distinctive in flavor because it's fortified with marc brandy, which inherently has lots of musky notes. There is a certain rawness to it that I adore, but it's softened by lovely notes of honey and wildflowers.

Pineau des Charantes
An apéritif wine made by combining and aging a mixture of unfermented grape juice and Cognac.

Quite honestly, I don't know what I was doing or who I was before I discovered Pineau des Charantes. This revelation completely changed my cocktail game. This aperitif wine is what you'll find farmers sipping in the French countryside after a day of work. Delicious on the rocks or elongated by some bubbly water, it has a texture so dreamy, a raisiny taste so enveloping, you might become so enamored that you'll find yourself wondering how this liquid gold is not drunk by every single person on earth on a daily basis. Full of caramel notes, but not in a cloyingly sweet way, it's an absolute delight when accompanied by a piece of hard, salty cheese or, in my opinion, with a scoop of vanilla ice cream.

Pommeau
An apéritif wine made by combining and aging a mixture of apple juice, and sometimes pear juice, with Calvados.

Like with my Arizona Tea comparison, I mean this in the best way possible, because I have no shame in saying that I love this stuff, but to me pommeau is like Martinelli's for big kids. Same mouthfeel, same vibrant and balanced acidity, and both benefit from being spritzified. It's a bottle with great versatility. Use a generous two-ounce pour and make it the main attraction or use it as a modifier to lift up other ingredients.

Some of My Faves

- **Château de Ravignan White Floc de Gascogne:** The texture of this wine is so gorgeous; it coats your mouth in a truly magical way. Lots of cantaloupe, lots of honey, complemented by little spurts of bright lemon peel.

- **Domaine Rolet Red Macvin du Jura:** Made from organically farmed grapes, this fortified wine is surprisingly acidic and full of those earthy, funky notes you crave from an MDJ.

- **Pierre Ferrand Pineau des Charantes:** Raisins, raisins, and more raisins. If booze were to take cookie form, this would be a golden-brown oatmeal raisin cookie without necessarily being confectionary. Also a great bargain for your buck!

- **Lemorton Pommeau:** Lemorton makes some of my favorite Calvados, so it's no surprise that their pommeau is terrific as well. I'm obsessed with the tartness of this bottle, which makes it feel like biting into a juicy apple.

- **Neversink Apple Apéritif:** Technically not a Pommeau de Normandie, as it's not made in Calvados, Neversink Spirits from upstate New York makes this delightful take on the classic. They work alongside a local farm and brewery, cultivating ingredients specifically for their booze. Waste from the distillation process is recycled back to the farm as compost and animal feed. And, yes, it's delicious.

WHAT GETS REFRIGERATED AND WHAT DOESN'T? Fortified wines, like wine and unlike full-proof spirits, are not shelf-stable. Anything with an ABV of 20 percent or lower should live in the fridge. Once opened, fortified wines will last up to three weeks. Will they grow mold and explode? Absolutely not. But their dynamic flavor profile will start to deteriorate, leaving you with a sort of lingering musky aftertaste. Keeping track of what bottle was opened when can be impossible, so once I open a bottle, I grab my handy-dandy Sharpie and date the back of the bottle. Also, if you find yourself moving through a bottle slowly, many make excellent wine substitutes in cooking. Or maybe take it as a sign to host a little shindig and throw the bottle into a punch.

GRAIN-BASED, MOSTLY

PASTIS
A liqueur made by macerating star anise along with other herbs and barks into a neutral spirit, which is then mixed with sugar.

Okay, so pastis breaks the mold a little. Unlike other apéritifs, this one has an ABV ranging from 40 to 45 percent; however, it is drunk like an apéritif because it is traditionally enjoyed in the ratio of one part pastis to five parts chilled water, thus bringing its ABV down significantly. Pastis is often described as absinthe's little cousin. Yes, they are similar in color. Yes, both liquids are drunk diluted with water and become cloudy. Yes, they both taste a lot like licorice. However, what makes absinthe absinthe (besides the fact that it is overproof) is the addition of wormwood, which pastis does not count as an ingredient. The experience of pastis is like drinking a tall, cold glass of anise- and peppermint-infused water. It's got an unmistakably viscous mouthfeel, and although I'm now realizing that the way I describe it kind of sounds like drinking toothpaste, it's undeniably refreshing.

Some of My Faves

- **Henri Bardouin:** Counting more than sixty-five different spices and herbs in its recipe, I love this bottle primarily because of its warming undertones of cardamom and cinnamon.

- **Argalá:** A pastis made in Italy—Piedmont to be more exact—this has a truly unique taste, mixing traditional alpine herbs with Mediterranean spices.

SAKE

An alcoholic brew from Japan made from polished fermented rice.

The first step in sake production is polishing and washing the rice. The polishing process is a delicate one and is indicative of how "premium" the sake is. The milled clean rice is then steamed. In order to turn rice into alcohol, one must add *koji*, which is a mold spore. This magical mold is able to break down the starches in the rice and convert them into sugar so it can then be fermented with the addition of yeast. There are endless varieties of sake, from filtered to unfiltered; some are best served warm, some are best serve chilled, some are fortified (although in sake land this signals it's of lesser quality), and some are even bubbly. The more polished the rice, the more "refined," or fancy, the sake. Although it is inherently dry, I find that sake has a sort of pudding-like quality to it. Perhaps I'm so tied up in the nostalgia of it all that I also associate it with a childhood treat, but seriously, if vanilla tapioca pudding could be an alcoholic beverage, it would be sake.

Some of My Faves

- **Kiku-Masamune, Junmai Kimoto:** This is a perfect all-around sake, great mixed into a cocktail and delicious served both chilled and warm (the way it is often drunk on Japanese New Year in my family). It's full of earthy umami flavors.

- **Rihaku-Shuzo, "Dreamy Clouds" Tokubetsu Junmai Nigori:** *Nigori* means that this sake is unfiltered, giving it that cloudy look. Richer, nuttier, slightly sweeter, it's also bursting with fruity plum notes to balance out that velvety mouthfeel.

UMESHU

A Japanese liqueur made by steeping ume in a mixture of neutral base spirit, such as sake or shochu and sugar.

Ume fruit is related to apricots and plums, but flavor-wise doesn't have much in common with either. Ume is known for its high citric acid content, and in fact while other fruit sweeten as they ripen, ume becomes more and more acidic. In its application, I like to think of it in the same way that I would use a sweet vermouth. And I encourage you to make your next Manhattan with umeshu, because it is divine!

Some of My Faves

- **Aoki Shuzu, Kakurei Ume-Shu Junmai Ginjo:** With a sake base, this bottle achieves the perfect balance of sweet and tart. Fun fact is that they use naturally derived rock candy as the sugar for this.

- **Umenoyado Brewery, Aragoshi Umeshu:** Also using a sake base, this umeshu is made a little differently and uses freshly squeezed ume plum juice. Aragoshi translates to "roughly pressed," which is evident in its cloudy, almost pulpy appearance. This bottle has a beautiful round mouthfeel that adds wonderful texture to a cocktail.

ALL THAT BITTER STUFF

BITTER GENTIAN LIQUEURS

A neutral base that has been infused and macerated with a variety of barks and herbs, specifically ones with a strong gentian presence; sugar is added but the result still maintains a subtle bitterness.

Some might say these bottles fall under the amaro category, but while many amari count gentian as an ingredient, these apéritif liqueurs make a very specific kind of bitterness their tagline. A little nip of these and your mouth is literally salivating, in a good way. A very good way.

Some of My Faves

- **Suze Apéritif:** One could say that I worship at the house of Suze. It's like an earthy, dirty, bitter lemon-drop candy—the finest compliment I think I've ever come up with.

- **Salers Gentian Apéritif:** Think of this gorgeous bottle as Suze's shy cousin. While gentian is certainly the predominant flavor here, alpine florals add an ethereal touch.

HERBAL BITTERS

Also known as amaro (Italian for "bitter"), these spirits also have a neutral base that has sugar added to it and has been infused and macerated with a variety of barks and herbs.

This category is enormous and varied with one common denominator—acute bitterness. Although softened with sugar, there is no denying that these bottles are chock-full of complex ingredients. Some amari are more subtle, while others get straight to the point and don't leave much to the imagination. Depending on their viscosity and level of bitterness, they can be fantastic as a full two-ounce pour for the base of your cocktail or, conversely, as a mere teaspoon to help highlight other flavors.

Some of My Faves

- **Branca Menta:** While you won't find me sipping this neat, although I know many people who find great joy in doing so, I love using this earthy, minty amaro in tiny little proportions to help lift and brighten heavy, dark ingredients.

  IF YOU LIKE BRANCA MENTA, TRY:
  - **Letherbee Fernet**
  - **Braulio**
  - **Averna**

- **Amaro Meletti:** Veering on the more viscous side, this bitter is all about caramelized orange peel and saffron, which helps to dry out and balance the sugar content.

  IF YOU LIKE AMARO MELETTI, TRY:
  - **Paolucci Amaro Cio Ciaro**
  - **Montenegro Amaro**
  - **Del Capo Amaro**
  - **Amaro Nonino**

- **Amaro Ramazzotti:** Full of rich berry notes, this makes me think of a complex jam.

  IF YOU LIKE AMARO RAMAZZOTTI, TRY:
  - Zucca
  - Amaro di Angostura

PINKY-ORANGE BITTERS

A neutral base spirit that has been infused and macerated with a variety of barks and herbs and has sugar added to it, while still maintaining subtle bitterness.

Some people might skewer me for this, but I'm making a separate little family for Aperol and Co., and for the purposes of this, I'm going to differentiate them by calling these bitter apéritifs "pinky-orange" versus "red." While many like to lump Aperol and Campari together, I argue that while they are similar in style, and by that I mean they both classify as a bitter apéritif, they are substantially different. Pinky-orange bitters are lighter, less bitter, far more citrusy, and lower in ABV than the red family.

Some of My Faves

- **Contratto Aperitif:** Slightly more bitter and drier than Aperol, this bottle has pleasantly surprising vegetal undertones and lovely little hints of tart rhubarb.
- **Rondo Spritz:** This organically farmed bitter is bursting with strawberry and wildflower notes while still remaining grounded, earthy, and, yes, sublimely bitter.

RED BITTERS

A neutral base spirit that has been infused and macerated with a variety of barks and herbs and has sugar added to it, while still maintaining intense bitterness. Historically made red by the addition of carmine dye derived from beetles, most are now colored with food dye.

The most famous bottle in this category is obviously Campari. And while we most certainly love ourselves some Campari, we shouldn't shut the door on the wide array of other bitter reds out there. Some are full-bodied, some light, some super floral, others grounded and earthy.

Some of My Faves

- **Forthave Spirits Red Aperitivo:** Using as many organically farmed ingredients as possible, including organic sugar, this Brooklyn-made red bitter is light and bursting with chamomile.
- **St. George Bruto Americano:** Like the name suggests, this one is go big or go home. Very bitter. Very citrusy. But with an unexpected plot twist—its finish is sublimely floral.
- **Cappelletti Vino Aperitivo:** Made with a wine base instead of a grain alcohol base, this delightful bitter clocks in at 17 percent ABV and was quite literally born to be turned into a spritz. If Campari is your thick night cream, this is your light all-day moisturizer.

LIFE'S SIMPLE PLEASURES Aren't you just in awe of all of these bottles?! Maybe feeling a little overwhelmed? That's okay! A wonderful thing to know about most of these is that they are magnificent in a simple one-and-one highball and that they all love being topped with something bubbly. Enjoying them like this or even just poured over some ice is a great way to get to know and appreciate this part of the liquor store. A pro tip to make those more viscous herbal bitters and liqueurs take themselves less seriously? Add a little float of them to your next poolside swim-up bar Piña Colada.

The Modifiers

I'm here to turn your world upside down. And I think you're going to like it. Your gins, your vodkas, your tequilas are the modifiers in this universe. That is to say, they are the supporting characters. So, they are vital because everyone needs a sidekick, but full-proof booze, if I even use it in a recipe, is there to add a little structure, texture, or pizzazz. In cooking terms, I really think of these bottles as the binding agent, as that touch of cream or that little squeeze of tomato paste. Dishes would feel incomplete sans these small additions. Without them, you'd be left wanting more, and not in that good way. I'm also going to approach this section a little differently than the last one and assume that most of you have somewhat of a foundation regarding these spirits. I've really sort of oversimplified what each category is defined as, so rather than bore you with production processes, I'm going to share with you how I incorporate full-proof spirits into my low-alcohol cocktails. Additionally, the specific brands or markers I'm highlighting in this section are what I consider workhorses. By that I mean they are quality bottles, at a great affordable value. If you want to use your $100-plus bottle of mezcal in one of my recipes, *absolutely* be my guest. But I'm here to offer you an alternative with a selection that I use for many of my bar projects. So let's get started. Get ready to see some of your familiar friends in a new light.

AQUAVIT
A neutral grain spirit that has been infused with caraway.

I realize I've used the word *love* a lot in this book already, but I really do love aquavit. This delectable liquid is all about savory culinary notes. I quite literally think of aquavit as seasoning in my low-ABV recipes. An aged aquavit like Linie is round and full of stone-fruit that complement the savory bite of the caraway, while unaged Krogstad is almost like chewing on fresh licorice bark, very green and bold and in your face.

BRANDY AND EAU DE VIE
A spirit distilled from fruit and or vegetables.

Oh, brandy. I wish I could write you a poem. Brandy is like that person you dated who not only brought you the most stunning bouquet of flowers, gave you the last bite of dessert, and ran you an almost sizzling-hot bubble bath but was *also* fantastic in bed. Brandy is full of surprises. Yeah, you've got your reliable standbys like Cognac and Calvados, but have you ventured into the wild and dynamic world of carrot eau de vie or American cherry brandy?! While cognacs such as Pierre Ferrand Ambre can add a luscious layer of crème brûlée to your cocktail, a teaspoon of Clear Creek Pear Brandy will make you feel like you are standing in a fruit orchard, biting into a just picked pear with juices running down your arm.

GIN
A neutral spirit flavored with botanicals, one of which must be juniper.

Nowadays we have a vast ocean of gins available to us, from the big guys to small local artisanal ones. I'll reach for a classic London Dry such as Tanqueray when I want to add a higher pitch to a cocktail, and by that I mean when the drink is full of heavy base notes and needs a brightening agent. If I want to add fullness, I depend on little splashes of gins like Perry's Tot, which is high in proof and has an almost lactic texture.

MEZCAL
A spirit made from a variety of agave plants, which are cooked underground.

Not only does mezcal impart a smoky, slightly charred flavor, it also adds (don't take this the wrong way) a sort of gasoline-like flavor. There is something very raw and, yes, reminiscent of petrol about mezcal. That intensity can stand up to equally strong characters such as hops or spice. Vida Mezcal is a great go-to bottle, and if I'm looking for something a little more subtle and sweet, I reach for Los Vecinos.

NATURAL FRUIT LIQUEURS
A neutral spirit that has added sugars and has been infused and/or macerated with fruit.

There are a lot of imposters in this category, and seeking out fruit liqueurs made from real wholesome fruit is vital to make this worth your while. Like with herbal liqueurs, a little bit can go a long way and completely transform your cocktails. I also love using fruit liqueurs because unlike fresh fruit (and don't get me wrong, I LOVE fresh fruit in cocktails), they are shelf-stable, so in the middle of a New York winter I can get strawberries into my drink without flying them in from California. You'll often find me splitting these with another sweetener, such as simple syrup, in a recipe. You can't go wrong with the entire line from Giffard, although I'm particularly fond of their passion fruit and peach liqueurs. Also, a huge fan of Current Cassis, which really is a hybrid between a fruit and herb liqueur and drinks more like a vermouth, so don't go into this expecting a viscous syrup. This lovely concoction is made with lightly fermented New York–grown black currants, wild honey, and lemon verbena, and it is yum.

RUM
A spirit made from molasses.

RHUM
A spirit made from raw sugar cane juice.

The thing about rum is that it is so varied! White rums offer a clean, bright tropical-fruit note, while a fifteen-year aged Demerara rum can present flavors such as caramelized banana and dark chocolate. And then you've also got rhum, which right off the bat is much grassier and wild; throw it in a barrel and you've got hay and nuttiness. Rum is definitely something I reach for when I'm looking to fold in an extra layer of depth. Smith & Cross Jamaican Rum is like a tropical Christmas cookie in liquid form, and Rhum JM Blanc likens itself to an almost overly ripe guava. For bright, grassy rum, I reach for Copalli, which is also organically grown and sustainably made. So basically, if you are not already drinking lots of r(h)um, you should start, because the lexicon is vast.

SUPER HERBAL LIQUEURS
A neutral spirit that has added sugars and has been infused and/or macerated with a variety of proprietary herbs.

With these complex liqueurs you can add layers upon layers of flavor with just a tiny flick of the wrist. While they are liqueurs, meaning they have sugar added for sweetness, all are inherently vegetal and savory. The grand madam of this category is Chartreuse; both green and yellow are bold and big. For a more quiet take, I always love a swig of génépi made from alpine herbs. And then there's Liquore Strega, laced with saffron and mint, a real mood-lifter in my opinion.

TEQUILA
A spirit made from steamed 100 percent Blue Weber agave.

Blanco Tequila can add crisp green flavors. Siembra Azul Blanco reminds me of biting into a green bell pepper while sitting on a just-cut lawn. Fortaleza Reposado Tequila makes me think of toasted coriander and cinnamon, and finally there's El Tesoro

Añejo Tequila, which reminds me of roasted poblano peppers and creamy vanilla. No matter the age, tequila is a brightening agent to me.

VODKA
A neutral spirit that can be made from anything from wheat to apples to potatoes.

When I use vodka in one of my low-ABV cocktails, it's often to level it out without necessarily changing its flavor much. Perhaps it's lacking body, so I depend on something like Grey Goose to add richness and a bite. And then there are vodkas like Roku, which add a soft, almost floral note that can help round out sharp corners. I also love Good Vodka, which is made from discarded cascara scraps left over from coffee production and is produced in such a way that it is carbon negative, and its almost oily texture can add wonderful viscosity to a drink.

WHISKEY
A spirit distilled from wheat, rye, or other grains.

Whiskey is obviously a huge category that includes bourbon, rye, scotch, Japanese whiskey, and more. Bourbon is made from predominantly corn, while rye is made of at least 51 percent rye, scotch can see the addition of peat, and Japanese whiskey is all about the water they use. But one thing I find common to all whiskeys is that there is something very grounding about them. If I feel like my cocktail note is too high, I know that Elijah Craig Bourbon can bring it back down to earth. Rittenhouse Rye will add an ultra-drying and almost peppery quality, while Suntori Toki whiskey delicately levels things out with hints of apricot pit.

Little Helpers

So you've dreamt up a cocktail concept with two ounces of Pommeau and a teaspoon of mezcal—what next?! Will this drink be a fruit-forward highball topped with bubbles or an intoxicating indulgence with some aromatic bitters? Whether it's a generous pour of bitter tonic water or a squeeze of brightening citrus juice, these are the ingredients that lend a helping hand and allow a cocktail to take form.

BUBBLY TOPPERS

Bubbles are all about elongating a delicious experience. Adding effervescence to a cocktail automatically adds an element of fun, because a well-structured bubble has the ability to dance on your tongue. Yes, you just read the phrase *well-structured bubble* because, believe it or not, bubbles

are not all created equal, and the quality of bubble can have a significant effect on the enjoyability of your drink. Bubbles stay bubblier when cold, so as a general note to this section, make sure that you always give whatever topper you are using a healthy chill!

BITTER SODAS

What I love about bitter sodas is that they feel like a complete cocktail in and of themselves. Sprucing them up with a little nip of sherry feels a bit like sneaking out of gym class to make out with someone. While most are inherently on the sweeter side, there's nothing like a little jolt of sugar to get those butterflies going.

Some of My Faves . . .

- **San Bitter:** This adorable little bottle that pretty much tastes like a nonalcoholic Campari and Soda has been my go-to soda since I was a teenager visiting my dad in Italy.

- **Casamara Club Amaro Sodas:** These über-dry (!!!) sodas are refreshing and whimsical while also managing to be completely sophisticated.

- **Chinotto:** Made from an orange variety known as a myrtle-leaved orange, this soda is bitter, salty, and full of tannins that really activate your taste buds.

SELTZER AND MINERAL WATER

To me, seltzer is a neutral lengthener. But just because I use the word *neutral,* I don't want you to think "boring," because good, mineral-rich bubbly water has the ability to add an entire new dimension, whether to a cocktail with five ingredients or to a simple one-and-one highball. And as a quick clarification between seltzer and sparkling mineral water, seltzer is force-carbonated water that does not contain salt; sparkling mineral water comes from a natural underground spring high in minerals, and its carbonation is often naturally occurring, although sometimes it's added. And then of course there is also club soda, which is seltzer with the addition of mineral salts.

Some of My Faves

- **Topo Chico:** This mineral-rich sparkling water from Mexico has amassed an almost cult-like following in the cocktail community, and for good reason. Its bubbles are vibrant, to put it mildly, and can almost make your eyes water. Legend has it that it has healing properties.

- **Canada Dry Seltzer:** No-frills, good old reliable seltzer water. I prefer buying the little 375 ml glass bottles—perfect size for a couple of drinks, and they are resealable, so they'll stay bubbly for a couple of hours.

- **Vichy Catalan Mineral Water:** This bottle is salty. Like, full-on salty sparkling water. It contains 1 gram of sodium per liter. This stuff brings me right back to my childhood in Germany, where my best friend's family loved drinking *Saltzwasser*. The bubbles in Vichy aren't aggressive, they're just right, and while I don't recommend this as a substitute for non-extra-sodium-laced water, there are some drinks that literally scream for this (says the lady who requests extra salt for her salt rims).

SPARKLING WINES

When choosing a sparkling wine for a cocktail I always look for two things: (1) it must be dry, and (2) it must have a tight bubble structure. While prosecco is a perfectly wonderful addition to any cocktail and a sort of no-brainer, cost-effective choice for bars, there's a huge and exciting world of bubbly wines to choose from.

Some of My Faves

- **Rheingau Sekt:** This has been my go-to bubbly wine topper bottle for years now! Organically farmed, this wine is wonderfully dry, full of expressive bubbles, and mind-blowingly affordable. They also make an equally delightful sparkling rosé that I can't recommend enough.

- **Regnier-David Cremant de Loire Rosé NV:** Tart strawberries prevail in this organically farmed bubbly. Perfect little bubbles aplenty.

TONIC WATER

One half of the eponymous duo Gin and Tonic, this soda is made of sparkling water, sugar, and quinine, which gives tonic its distinctive bitter taste. Like many other booze or booze-akin ingredients, quinine, which is derived from the chinchona tree, was used for medicinal purposes, as it can help ease an upset stomach and treat malaria. Tonic water is horribly underused, which I attribute to people thinking it's that syrupy flat goop that comes out of a soda gun. In reality it is beyond versatile and refreshing and I encourage you to become a tonic water snob.

Breaking the Mold

Tradition, schmadition. Cocktails are all about fun and self-expression, so feel free to venture out and take advantage of the enormous array of sparkling beverages out there! Kombucha—yep, it can be terrific in a drink! Niche flavored seltzer—yup! Here are some untraditional bubblies I've stumbled upon that have seriously upped my cocktail game.

ROSEHILL FARM BELLE DU NORD CIDER: This sustainably farmed cider is made five minutes from where I live, and during the summer months you can find me in their orchards, reveling among the gorgeous fruit they are growing. This dry and wild fermented sparkling cider is obviously wonderful on its own but is also a perfect addition to an avant-garde spritz.

BUNNY SPARKLING YUZU SAKE: Drinking this makes me giddy. Created with the juice and zest of yuzu, this sake gains its effervescence from in-bottle fermentation. They also make a peach and blueberry version that I'm very fond of as well.

OTHERS TO CONSIDER: Beer, commercial sodas (yes, Coke and Fanta can be pretty great at times!). Have you tried ume-laced seltzer?! Just please no energy drinks!

Some of My Faves

- **Fever Tree Indian Tonic Water:** To me this is the benchmark of what tonic can be! Fever Tree makes a wonderful line of tonics with a huge range of expressions and flavors, all delicious—this is the bottle to reach for when you want a classic G&T.

- **Q Tonic Water:** This one is all about its bubble content. It's not only very effervescent, but the bubbles also last and keep your drink bubbly from first sip to last. Q is also on the drier side.

- **Canada Dry Tonic Water:** This is no-frills tonic water, but it's totally dependable and available; every gas station in the country stocks it.

JUICE

All juice in this book is freshly squeezed or extracted, unless otherwise noted in the recipe. Additionally, all juice should be double-strained either through a superbag or chinois to achieve ultimate silky texture. It goes without saying that fruit should come from healthy fruit and veggies, organic if possible (not because of some sort of elitist attitude but rather as a way to preserve the health of our planet), and recipes calling for seasonal fruit or veggies are best made during their peak ripeness, not just to ensure best possible flavor but also as a way of showing your appreciation for nature. The recipes in this book call for the following:

- **Beet juice**
- **Bell pepper juice (red and green)**
- **Blood orange juice**
- **Carrot juice**
- **Celery juice**
- **Cucumber juice**
- **Ginger root juice**
- **Grapefruit juice**
- **Lemon juice**
- **Lime juice**
- **Orange juice**
- **Pineapple juice**
- **Watermelon juice**

ENHANCERS

Sometimes you construct what seems *should* be a perfect cocktail, but sip after sip leaves you feeling somehow unsatisfied, like something is missing. Here are three ingredients in my arsenal that I use to help bridge the gap.

3 PERCENT SALT SOLUTION: A simple yet highly impactful solution of kosher salt and water. I keep this simple yet highly impactful solution of kosher salt and water around in a dropper bottle. Just as in food, salt helps bring out flavors, accentuate nuances, and draw out layers that would otherwise go unnoticed. Just a few drops can help make a flabby cocktail (sorry for the gross visual) feel structured. I tell you how to make it on page 261.

CITRIC ACID: I use this in two ways: as a citric acid solution in a dasher bottle to add to cocktails in drop form, and as an ingredient in some syrups. In liquid form, it's a wonderful way to add a little touch of tartness to a cocktail that doesn't contain citrus juice. The tartness derived from citric acid is much more laser-focused than the one derived from juice. In pure powder form, citric acid is a great way to add brightness to cooked fruit syrups, as that sparkle from fresh fruit is often lost.

LACTIC ACID: Derived from sour dairy products, lactic acid not only adds acidity but also texture. I love to use this powder to ramp up the implied mouthfeel in syrups.

EXTRACTS

Natural extracts are a fantastic and efficient way to add unexpected flavor to a cocktail. I love browsing on Terra Spice's website for eternal inspiration. For the recipes in this book I use the following:

- **Cola extract**
- **Eucalyptus extract**
- **Orange extract**
- **Root beer extract**
- **Vanilla extract**

JAMS AND MARMALADES

I often joke that Bonne Maman should sponsor me. It's not really a joke because seriously, I am proud to be living that fruit-preserve life! Jams are my go-to for a few reasons.

- **They help us with texture problems, helping give thin cocktails that much needed rounded boost.**

- **They're a great way to add fruit even when they are out of season.**

- **They don't really spoil! We love things that last!**

- **Jams are easy to make and are a wonderful by-product of some of our fruit syrups (yup, those leftover raspberries that have been steeping in simple syrup are a fab start to your morning routine).**

BITTERS

Treat bitters bottles the way you would treat spice jars in your kitchen. Bitters are a little more exciting because they are basically proprietary unique spice *blends*. And I've gotta say, what a time to be alive, because there are so many good bitters options on the market. But don't necessarily be like a trigger-happy cook in the kitchen, adding a little pinch of this and a little pinch of that, and a little pinch of this and that until you have a hodgepodge something that doesn't really taste like one thing or another. Bitters are best used with a bit of restraint. They are after all teeny-tiny flavor bombs.

AROMATIC BITTERS: These include our trusty friends Angostura and Peychaud. Filled to the brim with barks, spices, and citrus peels, they lean on the more, ahem, bitter side, counting such things as gentian root and chinchona bark among their ingredients. Aside from these two pantry staples, I love Bitter Truth Jerry Thomas Bitters, which are basically a clove and cinnamon explosion. Bitter End makes some incredible flavor combinations, but I'm very partial to their Moroccan bitters that are full of coriander and mint. And I have to give Miracle Mile Castilian Bitters a big shout-out because they make everything taste better.

CITRUS BITTERS: When I started working behind bars, the only citrus bitters I had ever seen were orange. Now there's everything from grapefruit to black lemon (Scrappy's makes an excellent one) to yuzu (Miracle Mile is our go-to for this). As you would expect, these add a lovely little hit of brightness.

SPICY BITTERS: Not all cocktails call for green jalapeño, a lesson I wish more drink creators would embrace. There are so many types of spice and bitters are a wonderful way to explore them. Bitter End makes a truly delicious Curry Bitters, which gets its heat from both cayenne and black pepper. Who can forget about Miracle Mile's Chocolate Chili Bitters, which helps add stunning curves to a drink.

STONE FRUIT BITTERS: These are our cherries, apricots, and peaches. Flavors that are somehow both grounding and elevating. Our trusty friends at Miracle Mile make ume bitters that pretty much sing to me. Cecil & Merl make both delightful apricot and sour cherry versions.

NUTTY BITTERS: From toasted pecan to hazelnut and green walnut, these bitters are natural companions to aged whiskeys and brandies, but pair them with sherry or madeira and find yourself with a heavenly match.

EARTHY BITTERS: While not an actual "category"—in fact, most people might place them in the aromatic column—I like to distinguish these based on their ability to add a certain grit to cocktails. Dram Apothecary makes a gorgeous alcohol-free Palo Santo bitters, which, by the way, is ethically sourced. Cecil & Merl makes a matcha bitters that has the ability to add a rugged floral note to your cocktails (I know, rugged and floral don't usually go hand in hand, but trust me).

Ice

It's an ingredient. Once you start treating it as such, you'll understand why bartenders are so obsessed with "the right kind of ice." We add dilution, aka water, to our cocktails by either shaking or stirring the ingredients together. Adding the right amount of water while simultaneously reaching the perfect temperature is the delicate balance we are all after. So, let's say we are shaking a Daiquiri—rum, lime juice, sugar—and using crappy deli ice. You'll only be able to shake it for a few seconds before turning that mixture into a watery mess, and now you won't be able to reach that bracingly cold temperature either. Shake it long enough to achieve that frosty bliss and you've effectively smashed all the crappy ice, turning your drink into overly diluted slush. On the other side of mixing up your concoction is the ice your drink is served over. You want your drink to hold on to its temperature and its dilution ratio while also acknowledging that it's a victory-less battle, so, rather than fall over in defeat, accept the realities of impending cocktail death and try and slow down the process. And this is where ice quality comes into question.

At bars and restaurants, we have fancy industrial machines to make the majority of our ice for us, but at home, all you need are some reusable silicone ice trays, or you can even give your plastic takeout containers a second life by freezing large ice blocks in them. Most fridges with ice makers have a crushed ice setting; otherwise, fill a sealable food-safe bag with ice cubes, wrap it in a towel, and put your hammer to work.

CUBED
1¼-inch by 1¼-inch cubes

Best for
- Shaking and stirring cocktails
- As ice in a highball or wineglass

CRUSHED
Pellets—can be rounded or squarish

Best for
- Whip shaking
- As ice in a double rocks, highball, wineglass, or festive glass

Speaking of crushed ice, you'll see me call for a technique I like to call "snow cone" in some of the cocktails served over crushed ice. Snow-coning is quite literally just creating a beautiful, hand-compacted, crushed ice mound on top of your drink.

LARGE FORMAT
2-inch by 2-inch cubes

Best for
- Shaking cocktails
- As ice in a double rocks glass

PRO TIP: To get that gorgeous layer of scrumptious frothy cocktail heaven and to give the drink an all-around glorious texture, I use the combination "large-format ice + 2 cubed ice cubes" for all of my shaken cocktails served up.

MEGA ICE
It can vary according to the size or shape of your serving vessel, but I'm talkin' a big old hunk of ice.

Best for
- Ice in a punch bowl

HACK: For ultimate party fun, there is nothing more spectacular than an embellished ice block floating in your punch. Whether you freeze in some edible flowers or make the ice sparkle with some food-grade iridescent luster dust, let your imagination run wild for maximum impact!

Garnish

A garnish should always be a considered decision, an ingredient that enhances a cocktail. It can be completely visual, such as an edible flower, or as simple as a lime wedge, but it must serve a purpose, even if completely superficial.

Let's take the lime wedge, for example. It's a garnish we see on so many cocktails, but I don't think most people give it much thought or consideration, and that drives me bananas. If you choose to garnish a cocktail with a lime wedge, you should be deliberate about it and consider the following: some people will squeeze it in, while others will completely disregard it. So, as drink creators, we have to make sure that the cocktail is equally delicious *with* the lime wedge squeezed in and *without*. If something comes with a lime wedge, I like to give the maker the benefit of the doubt and assume it was a deliberate choice— as should you. Now, garnishes don't always have to be practical. Garnishes are, in essence, an embellishment, so a paper umbrella is wonderful when it is appropriate. Edible glitter is never *not* appropriate. But let's get back to the lime wedge. Nothing irritates me more than being served a beautifully made, thoughtful cocktail in a stunning glass, only to see that the lime wedge on the rim of my perfectly delicate coupe is brown. GAH. Take the time to be intentional with the entirety of the drink, from your first dash of bitters to the deseeded lemon wheel garnish. With that, let's talk about some general garnish guidelines.

- **It should come from a healthy and vibrant source.**

- **It should not interfere with being able to enjoy the cocktail.**

- **Deseed any citrus.**

- **Store fresh leafy herbs, such as mint or basil, in a couple of inches of icy water upside down with leaves submerged.**

- **Trim stems before use.**

- **Keep olives, onions, and brandied cherries cold before plopping them into your cocktail.**

- **Always remove pith from citrus wedges, wheels, and crescents.**

- **Don't trim the ends/tips off citrus wedges! Let a lemon look like a lemon!**

- **Citrus fruit to be used for twists should be washed with warm water—no one wants the remnants of the back of your fridge squeezed into their drink.**

- **Citrus twists should have minimal pith.**

One Step at a Time

I like to think of assembling cocktails like a choreographed dance. A night of service, or a night at home with friends, can be unpredictable, so in order to keep my sanity (and stamina), I cling to the certainties of any given moment. This means that my bar station has a very specific setup, called mise en place, so that I could basically bartend with my eyes closed, or, in more practical terms, I can hold an immersive conversation with a guest while not missing a beat in my steps of service.

I build drinks in a specific order, I shake and stir in a specific order, every tool used immediately returns to its rightful home. Why? Because things will inevitably go wrong, so when the glass shatters on your bar top or the ice machine breaks down, I'm not adding additional pressure and panic to an already stressful situation by looking for my bar spoon. So how does this apply to making a casual spritz while barefoot and in the comfort of your own home? What I'm talking about is an almost ceremony-like approach to cocktail making, one that celebrates order and that will hopefully enable you to carry a spirit of calm into your creations.

When building your rounds of drinks, think of them in terms of stability. Basically, just as a hot dish out of an oven is battling the clock to stay warm before it is served and eaten, cocktails are also immediately faced with impending doom as they start deteriorating instantly. The goal is to keep hot drinks hot, cold drinks cold, and drinks served over ice not overly diluted. I, on my mother's side, stem from seventeen generations of Buddhist priests (didn't think I was gonna go there, did you?!), and although my sister and I weren't raised with a specific religion, I'm sure you can imagine that sort of lineage had an impact on how my mother raised my sister and me. Strangely, making cocktails, and the roads one must travel to make them, is inherently very Buddhist, as the idea of impermanence is at the forefront. Making cocktails can actually be a very cathartic process, because it forces you to accept that nothing lasts forever and that many things are out of our control. But do not translate that into a complacent and lazy acceptance of defeat. Quite the contrary. Cocktail making is not a passive endeavor. If anything, it should help you realize your ability and potential by actively engaging you in taking the steps to slow down the process of deterioration. In other words, embrace those steps that you can control, let go of unrealistic expectations, and let the good times roll. Thank you for indulging me there.

INSPIRED BY
THE GREATS:

USING
CLASSIC
COCKTAILS

THESE ARE THE RECIPE FORMULAS I RELY ON, THE BUILDING BLOCKS THAT ALLOW FOR CREATIVITY AND FREEDOM OF ARTISTIC EXPRESSION.

Like I always said to our staff at Nitecap—the reason we can have fun doing what we are doing is because we are confident in our abilities, which are based on a strong understanding of our foundation. Once these recipes make sense, it's all about manipulating them to develop new ones.

In my creative journey, I have found that giving myself parameters and structure actually allows me to think outside the box more. To organize my always jumbled mind, I like to think of cocktails as falling into certain categories. To pinpoint the category, I try to imagine what sort of void this drink is trying to fill. After all, do we ever really *need* new cocktails when there are already so many out there? If it's not a void I'm trying to fill (because, really, that's sort of an all-important way to look at it), I try to think about paying homage to cocktails that I adore. Either way, cocktail inception starts in the same place—a classic cocktail template.

Here are the seven formulas I look to. I should add that there are hundreds more recipes I could have included here, but I've narrowed them down in a way that I find helpful for the purposes of this specific book and the recipes I've chosen to fill these pages with.

The Sour

In its most basic form, the Sour is spirit, citrus, and a nonalcoholic sweetener, garnished with a citrus wedge.

Foundation Recipe

2 ounces spirit

¾ ounce fresh lemon or lime juice

½ ounce Simple Syrup (page 252)

Combine the spirit, lemon or lime juice, and syrup in shaker. Add ice and shake. Strain over fresh ice into a double rocks glass. Garnish with a wedge of lemon or lime.

Some Classic Sour Offspring

Daiquiri, Gimlet, Mojito, Piña Colada, Pisco Sour, Ramos Gin Fizz, Tom Collins, Whiskey Sour

The Daisy

In its most basic form, the Daisy is spirit, citrus, and a liqueur as sweetener, garnished with a citrus wedge or twists.

Foundation Recipe

2 ounces spirit

1 ounce orange curaçao

¾ ounce fresh lemon or lime juice

Combine the spirit, orange curaçao, and lemon or lime juice in a shaker. Add ice and shake. Strain into a coupe glass. Garnish with a citrus wedge or twist.

Some Classic Daisy Offspring

Corpse Reviver No. 2, Cosmopolitan, Mai Tai, Margarita, Sidecar, The Last Word

The Highball

In its most basic form, the Highball is spirit and bubbly lengthener, garnished with a citrus wedge or long twist.

Foundation Recipe

2 ounces spirit

4 ounces bubbly water

Combine the spirit and bubbly water in a highball glass filled with cubed ice. Gently stir ingredients to incorporate. Garnish with a citrus wedge or long twist.

Some Classic Highball Offspring
Whiskey Highball, Gin and Tonic, Moscow Mule, Rum and Coke, Kalimotxo, Americano, Pimm's Cup, Bloody Mary

The Spritz

In its most basic form, the spritz is wine-based spirit, sparkling wine, and bubbly nonalcoholic lengthener, garnished with a citrus wheel or crescent.

Foundation Recipe

2 ounces wine-based apéritif or wine

3 ounces sparkling wine

1 ounce bubbly water

Combine wine, sparkling wine, and bubbly water in a wineglass filled with ice. Gently stir to combine. Garnish with a citrus wheel or crescent.

Some Classic Spritz Offspring
White Wine Spritz, Aperol Spritz, French 75, Kir Royale

The Martini

In its most basic form, the Martini is spirit and vermouth, garnished with an olive or a twist (or if you're me, you garnish with an olive and a twist!).

Foundation Recipe

2 ounces spirit

1 ounce dry vermouth

Combine spirit and vermouth in a mixing glass. Add ice and stir. Strain into a Nick and Nora glass. Garnish with an olive or citrus twist.

Some Classic Martini Offspring
Gin Martini, The 50/50, Martinez, Manhattan, Negroni, Boulevardier, Vesper, Vieux Carré

The Old-Fashioned

In its most basic form, the Old-Fashioned is spirit, sugar, and bitters, garnished with orange and lemon twists.

Foundation Recipe

2 ounces spirit

1 teaspoon rich sugar syrup

2 dashes aromatic bitters

Combine the spirit, sugar syrup, and bitters in a mixing glass. Add ice and stir. Strain into a double rocks glass over large-format ice. Garnish with an expressed lemon twist and an orange twist.

Some Classic Old-Fashioned Offspring
Classic Old-Fashioned, Sazerac, Fancy Free, Mint Julep, Sherry Cobbler

The Alexander

In its most basic form, the Alexander is spirit, liqueur as sweetener, and heavy cream, garnished with freshly grated nutmeg.

Foundation recipe

1 ounce spirit

1 ounce sweet liqueur

1 ounce heavy cream

Combine the spirit, sweet liqueur, and heavy cream in a shaker. Add ice and shake. Fine-strain into a Nick and Nora glass. Garnish with freshly grated nutmeg.

Some Classic Alexander Offspring
Brandy Alexander, Coffee Cocktail, Barbary Coast

HOW TO CUSTOMIZE & CREATE

So now we have our foundations. I'm not the first to make this analogy, but one can think of creating new cocktail recipes as a booze-fueled game of Mr. Potato Head. In other words, take your foundation recipe and start dissecting it ingredient by ingredient. Who are the core players in each cocktail and how do you want to tell their story? Think of these core players as your "certains." By that I mean they are elements that must be in your cocktail to ensure they are balanced. Find comfort in these certainties, as they will serve as your guides. If you want to create, say, a Sour, you know for certain that your recipe must include an acidifier and a sweetener. How one chooses to balance them is the endless puzzle that keeps my mind, creativity, and hands active and engaged.

One glaring thing you may have noticed is that all the recipes I just listed as foundational are not necessarily low in alcohol. This is not an oversight or mistake—quite the opposite, actually. For many, apéritif culture is deeply rooted in the way it's always been done. That means defining low-ABV cocktails through a limited lens of one-and-one highballs and Aperol Spritzes (two drinks that I adore and drink frequently). Instead, this approach allows for more complex, creative results. So, yes, you'll hear me liken one of my cocktails to a stiff drink like a Manhattan, but rest assured, it won't have two full ounces of overproof rye whiskey.

GULPABLE THIRST QUENCHERS

You know that whole "makeup/no-makeup" look? Or that "how do they look *so cool* in a vintage T-shirt and jeans they just picked up off of the floor and threw on" vibe? Yeah, that's what these drinks are all about. They certainly require a little bit of behind-the-scenes work but come off as entirely effortless. If cocktails were colors, these would be the neon yellows, the fuchsias, coral blues, emerald greens, the lilacs laced with an iridescent shimmer. These are happy drinks. Drinks that punctuate a guttural laugh, accompany new-crush make-out sessions, and make even the mundane task of taking a shower seem like a genuine delight. Yes, I'm encouraging shower cocktails every now and again! This section is all about bright, sparkly, cheerful cocktails. They should invigorate the soul. I hope this chapter brings you the purest form of joy.

Refreshing, Tart, and Ultra-lighthearted, Drinks That Go Down Easy and Fill You with Life

Pinkies Out

Best enjoyed when . . . *cutting up peaches, barefoot, windows open, slight breeze*

Well, this is THE drink, the one that started this whole crazy journey, the inspired by but totally not White Wine Spritz. This cocktail was created for Nitecap's inaugural menu. I had set up a wine tasting with one of our reps who specialized in eastern European wines, and one sip of an unctuous, dry Slovenian bottle had me immediately thinking about putting it in a cocktail. The wine reminded me a lot of Lillet; with a floral nose and honey-like finish, it was begging to be spritzified. I know there are a lot of wine people rolling their eyes right now, but trust me, this cocktail is an homage to the wine, its maker, and my mother, and you don't want to insult my mother, right?!

Serves 1
Glassware: Wineglass
Ice: Cubed
Garnish: Orange crescent

2 ounces dry orange wine

1 ounce Cocchi Americano Bianco

1 ounce Chamomile Blanc Vermouth (page 258)

½ ounce white verjus

Dry hard sparkling cider, to top

Combine the orange wine, Cocchi Americano, chamomile-infused vermouth, and verjus in a wineglass filled with 3 hand-cracked ice cubes. Add more ice. Top with the hard cider. Stir to chill and incorporate all ingredients. Garnish with an orange crescent.

CRIMSON
SOUR,
PAGE 93

THROWBACK,
PAGE 94

GIGGLE FIT,
PAGE 95

Crimson Sour

Best enjoyed when . . . *contemplating your evening plans*

I'm one of those people who dreads winter. Yeah, yeah, snow is pretty, but I'd never willingly go play in it. That's what sand is for. But sitting by the fireplace is so romantic. (You know what's more romantic than sitting by a fireplace in a fleece pajama set? Sitting on a beach, topless, with sweat beads glistening on my bronzed skin as the sun shines down on me with all her glory.) I'll give winter one thing, though—citrus season. Ah, yes, the time of year when bright-hued Meyer lemons make regular old lemons hide with shame, when it's not just grapefruits but also pomelos and flame grapefruits. And, of course, the mighty blood orange in all its stain-inducing power. Besides being glorious to look at, it is beautifully sweet and possesses an intoxicating, almost overripe, raspberry taste. This recipe is built around highlighting all of the blood orange's gorgeous qualities.

Serves 1

Glassware: Double rocks

Ice: Crushed

Garnish: Blood orange crescent and lemon wheel

1½ ounces full-bodied sweet (red) vermouth

¾ ounce fresh lemon juice

¾ ounce fresh blood orange juice

½ ounce Cacao Nib Campari (page 259)

½ ounce Vanilla Syrup (page 255)

Combine the sweet vermouth, lemon juice, blood orange juice, cacao-infused Campari, and syrup in a shaker. Add ice and give it a short shake. Strain into a double rocks glass over crushed ice. Top with more ice and snow-cone it (see Speaking of Crushed Ice, page 77). Garnish with a blood orange crescent and lemon wheel. Serve with a straw.

Throwback

Best enjoyed when . . . *eating a cheese sandwich, crusts cut off*

This is basically like the best adult soda you've ever had. I grew up in a home where it was all health food all the time. While other kids in elementary school got cookies in their lunch boxes, I got licorice sticks. And I'm not talking about chewy, sweet licorice Twizzlers; I'm talking *literal* sticks, like branches from a licorice tree. Yeah, I was the biracial kid chewing on a stick. It went great (Mom—I know you had the best intentions!). So, you can imagine how little soda we drank. I got one Coca-Cola on my birthday, one Shirley Temple when we went to our favorite Chinese restaurant when we visited my grandmother each year, and one root beer float to accompany burgers at our yearly pilgrimage to Smokehouse. I treated that root beer float as if God had presented herself to me in drink form. To this day, an ice-cold root beer, preferably over a mountain of crushed ice, is my favorite soda treat. But now I'm a big girl, so here is my adult version of soda.

Serves 1
Glassware: Highball
Ice: Cubed
Garnish: Lemon wedge

2 ounces Suze apéritif
¾ ounce fresh lemon juice
½ ounce Honey Syrup (page 253)
2 drops root beer extract
Bubbly water, to top

Combine the Suze, lemon juice, syrup, and root beer extract in a shaker. Add ice and shake. Strain into a highball glass over cubed ice. Top with the bubbly water. Give the drink a quick stir to incorporate all ingredients. Garnish with a lemon wedge. Serve with a straw.

Caution: Although it may seem tempting to just sub in some root beer soda from the deli downstairs, this drink won't be the same! The combination of bubbly water + root beer extract has the opposite effect of soda pop—it's supremely dry—thus making this drink refreshing and chuggable.

Giggle Fit

Best enjoyed when . . . *the one thing missing from your outfit is some ruffle*

I was first introduced to aquavit when I joined the opening team of Vandaag, an ambitious Scandinavian restaurant with one of the best, in my humble opinion, bar programs ever created. At the helm of the bar was Katie Stipe, a true mentor and now dear friend. I hadn't ever given aquavit much thought before, but Katie's application of it made me see it in a whole new light. Now, I have a lot of feelings about aquavit—adoration, love, obsession, to name a few. It's bright yet also intensely earthy and can be dressed up to look either very serious or playful and carefree. As the flavor profile of aquavit is very bold, it needs equally intense flavors to play with, and so I immediately reached for my bottle of carrot eau de vie. Oh, you don't have a bottle of carrot eau de vie lying around? Well, you should, because it's magic in a bottle. Each sip of carrot eau de vie takes you on a literal journey of eating a carrot that's been freshly plucked from the ground—you get the dirt, the bitterness of the carrot tops, and the sweet almost candy-like flavor of the flesh.

Serves 1

Glassware: Coupe

Ice: None

Garnish: Lemon twist

1 ounce Lillet Rosé

¾ ounce unaged aquavit (preferably Krogstad)

½ ounce fresh lemon juice

½ ounce Pomegranate Grenadine (page 252)

1 teaspoon Honey Syrup (page 253)

1 teaspoon Reisetbauer carrot eau de vie

Dry sparkling rosé, to top

Combine the Lillet Rosé, aquavit, lemon juice, pomegranate grenadine, syrup, and carrot eau de vie in a cocktail shaker. Add ice and shake. Fine-strain into a coupe glass. Top with the sparkling rosé. Garnish with an expressed lemon twist.

TELL ME MORE

I'll be totally up front with you, carrot eau de vie isn't exactly cheap. So if you're feeling a little funny spending the cash for 1 teaspoon in this recipe, I get it. But please know that besides adding a (yes, I'm sorry) teaspoon to your usual Martini, which is a game changer, this gift from nature is a treat drunk neat, chilled or at room temp.

Magic Moment

Best enjoyed when . . . *wanting to live a life less ordinary*

Call me crazy, but whenever I'm drinking an Aperol Spritz, I want to eat a beet salad. Also (and the Italians are going to ban me from their country for this), I want to garnish my Aperol Spritz with a grapefruit crescent rather than the recommended orange slice. Why? Because my palate craves bright, bitter, juicy citrus with the bittersweet voluptuous qualities of Aperol. To balance everything out, I picked pisco for its beautiful fragrant bouquet and to add a little *je ne sais quoi*. I'll be the first to admit that this drink reads strange, but trust me, it's a flavorful and nuanced sour. Yes, it requires a little more prep work than other recipes, but the result is worth it. Plus, you can always repurpose your bottle of beet-infused Aperol for a next-level Aperol Spritz.

Serves 1
Glassware: Double rocks
Ice: Large format
Garnish: Grapefruit crescent

1½ ounces Beet Aperol (page 258)

¾ ounce fresh grapefruit juice

¾ ounce Raspberry Syrup (page 255)

½ ounce fresh lime juice

½ ounce pisco

Combine the beet-infused Aperol, grapefruit juice, syrup, lime juice, and pisco in a cocktail shaker. Add ice and shake. Strain into a double rocks glass with large-format ice. Garnish with a grapefruit crescent.

Kitty Cat Chronicles

Best enjoyed when . . . *sitting cross-legged, in front of a backyard fire pit, toes exposed, blanket over shoulders*

If a cocktail could be a season, this one would be that little sliver in time at the end of summer: it's still sort of warm during the day, but a few leaves are starting to change color. You decided to cook your dinner on the grill, and finally, after months of sweating while manning the BBQ, you are perfectly comfortable, but once the sun sets, you have to put on a sweater. So, it's an homage to the almost too ripe fig that you've sneakily plucked from your neighbors (hey, the branch was technically on your property line) and the promise of ripe pears to come. And even though there is no single ingredient that is smoky, collectively this combination somehow ends up tasting toasty and grilled.

Serves 1

Glassware: Double rocks

Ice: Large format

Garnish: Pear fan on a cocktail pick

1½ ounces Lillet Rouge

¾ ounce Bonal Gentiane-Quina

¾ ounce fresh lemon juice

½ ounce Pomegranate Grenadine (page 252)

1 teaspoon unaged pear brandy (preferably Clear Creek)

1 heaping bar spoon of fig preserves

Combine the Lillet Rouge, Bonal, lemon juice, pomegranate grenadine, pear brandy, and fig preserves in a cocktail shaker. Add ice and shake. Fine-strain into a double rocks glass with large-format ice. Garnish with a pear fan on a cocktail pick.

Wiggle Room

Best enjoyed when . . . *yearning for a vacation but wanting to keep things a little familiar*

A Whiskey Highball and a Vermouth and Soda walk into a bar, fall in love, and elope to a tropical island. That's my sales pitch for this drink. But if you want to get a bit more in depth, I came up with this drink during my coconut obsession phase. I was *deep* into it at this point and wanted to make a Madeira Piña Colada, which never quite worked out, but I did discover that the flavor combination of madeira and coconut was a delightful one. The madeira here is infused with toasted coconut flakes, which also automatically gives the delicate wine more body, making it perfect for shaking up in a cocktail.

Serves 1
Glassware: Highball
Ice: Cubed
Garnish: Pineapple wedge

1½ ounces Toasted Coconut Madeira (page 259)

1 ounce Salted Lemon-Lime Cordial (page 253)

½ ounce bourbon

½ ounce fresh pineapple juice

Bubbly water, to top

Combine the toasted coconut–infused madeira, lemon-lime cordial, bourbon, and pineapple juice in a shaker. Add ice and give it a short shake. Strain into a highball glass with cubed ice. Top with the bubbly water. Stir to incorporate all ingredients. Garnish with a pineapple wedge. Serve with a straw.

Wildcat

Best enjoyed when . . . *wearing a large-brimmed hat and holding a small dog*

There is something insanely delicious about just-juiced carrot juice. Specifically, just-juiced carrot juice poured over a mountain of crushed ice. The flavor is intensely earthy with a hint of delectable sweetness. It's also slightly bitter, so it really just gets your taste buds working. I usually stay clear of cocktails I call "salad cocktails," that is, cocktails that have muddled this and muddled that and this herb and that herb and the juice of this vegetable and that vegetable. I guess you could say I overcame my own prejudice, and this is my version of a salad cocktail, completely making carrot juice the star.

Serves 1

Glassware: Festive

Ice: Crushed

Garnish: Cucumber slice (seedless), lavish mint bouquet, and cocktail umbrella

2 seedless cucumber slices

1½ ounces Pimm's

1½ ounces fresh carrot juice

¾ ounce fresh lemon juice

½ ounce Aperol

¼ ounce Ginger Syrup (page 254)

1 teaspoon Simple Syrup (page 252)

1 dash absinthe

Muddle the 2 cucumber slices at the bottom of a shaker. Add the Pimm's, carrot juice, lemon juice, Aperol, ginger syrup, simple syrup, and absinthe to the shaker. Add ice and shake. Fine-strain into a festive glass filled three-quarters with crushed ice. Top with more crushed ice and snow-cone it (see Speaking of Crushed Ice, page 77). Garnish with cucumber slice, lavish mint bouquet, and cocktail umbrella. Serve with a straw.

Smiley Smile

Best enjoyed when . . . *reminiscing on your party girl/boy/people days while wearing a towel turban and watching your nail polish dry*

This is a highball that gives you a little joyful shiver. The inspiration was the Gin and Tonic, and before you say anything, I know there is neither gin nor tonic in this recipe. This drink is kind of like method acting, a sensory experience guided by memory. Okay, I feel like I might be losing you, but stick with me. You're in a nightclub, the music is so loud you can feel it vibrating in your feet, there's strobe lights, you're sweaty, and your drink is empty. You make it up to the bar, the bartender is slammed, you want something refreshing, so you order a Gin and Tonic. The first sip is kind of overwhelming because it seems like you just took a huge gulp of gin and your tongue sort of tingles and feels a little numb, but in a pleasant way. A few sips in, the ingredients have mixed together and mellowed out. Yuzu does that same thing for me, and I love it!

Serves 1
Glassware: Highball
Ice: Cubed
Garnish: Long lemon twist

1 ounce manzanilla sherry

½ ounce Suze apéritif

½ ounce unaged pear brandy (preferably Clear Creak)

½ ounce fresh lemon juice

½ ounce Simple Syrup (page 252)

Sparkling yuzu sake, to top

Combine the sherry, Suze, pear brandy, lemon juice, and syrup in a cocktail shaker. Add ice and shake. Strain into a highball glass filled with cubed ice. Top with the sparkling yuzu sake. Stir to incorporate all ingredients. Garnish with a long expressed lemon twist. Serve with a straw.

Third Date

Best enjoyed when . . . *holding hands in an orchid-filled jungle*

To me, the third date was always the "all right, I'm definitely into you, I thought about what to wear since our last date, now tell me some of your dirty secrets and let's see if there is still a spark" date. In other words, you need a drink that (1) keeps you on your toes (you might need to run), (2) has some comforting flavors (exposing deep truths about yourself is scary), and (3) is delicious (because). So, cheers to your dating life and the utter craziness that is dating in the twenty-first century, and hopefully you want to make sweet, sweet love to this drink all night long.

Serves 1

Glassware: Double rocks

Ice: Large format

Garnish: Lemon wheel and cherry flag (see page 131)

1½ ounces sweet vermouth (preferably Carpano Antica)

¾ ounce fresh lemon juice

½ ounce sour cherry liqueur (preferably American Fruit Sour Cherry)

½ ounce Cinnamon Syrup (page 255)

¼ ounce Ancho Reyes Ancho Chile Liqueur

Combine the sweet vermouth, lemon juice, cherry liqueur, syrup, and Ancho Reyes in a shaker. Add ice and shake. Strain into a double rocks glass with large-format ice. Garnish with a lemon wheel and cherry flag.

TELL ME MORE

Why Carpano Antica in this recipe? We've already discussed how rich and decadent this sweet vermouth is, but it also has a nuanced hint of smoke that I think lends itself perfectly to this Whiskey Sour–inspired cocktail.

Endless Spring

Best enjoyed when . . . *incredibly parched*

This drink is beautifully simple and is all about the glorious strawberry. The cocktail calls for only half of a muddled strawberry, which may seem like so little, but this mighty berry is bursting with flavor. Another reason I can get away with using so little *actual* strawberry in this drink is because all the other ingredients bring out the strawberry-ness of that one little half. The Lillet Rosé is delicate and nuanced and reminds me of the stems and tops of a strawberry where there might still be a tiny bit of green. Amaro Ramazzotti, on the other hand, is deep and rich, voluptuous and ripe. And any strawberry worth talking about is equally as tart as it is sweet, thus the choice of lemon juice and a neutral sweetener such as simple syrup.

Serves 1
Glassware: Highball
Ice: Cubed
Garnish: ½ strawberry

½ strawberry
1 ounce Lillet Rosé
¾ ounce Amaro Ramazzotti
¾ ounce fresh lemon juice
½ ounce Simple Syrup (page 252)
Bubbly water, to top

Lightly muddle the ½ strawberry at the bottom of a shaker. Add the Lillet Rosé, Ramazzotti, lemon juice, and syrup to the shaker. Add ice and shake. Fine-strain into a highball glass with cubed ice. Top with the bubbly water. Stir to incorporate all ingredients. Garnish with the remaining strawberry half. Serve with a straw.

Serves 1

Glassware: Double rocks

Ice: Large format

Garnish: Pineapple wedge

1½ ounces Cola Lustau Rosé Vermut (page 258)

¾ ounce fresh pineapple juice

½ ounce Singani (preferably Singani 63)

½ ounce fresh lemon juice

¼ ounce maraschino liqueur (preferably Caffo)

¼ ounce Simple Syrup (page 252)

Combine the Cola Lustau Rosé Vermut, pineapple juice, Singani, lemon juice, maraschino liqueur, and syrup in a cocktail shaker. Add ice and shake. Strain into a double rocks glass with large-format ice. Garnish with a pineapple wedge.

Permission Slip

Best enjoyed when . . . *sitting on the floor of your living room after a night out with your partner(s) in crime*

A Rum and Coke is just so gloriously delicious sometimes. When I get that intense, albeit rare, craving for an ice-cold, bubbly, vanilla-y, cinnamon-y Coke, nothing can satisfy me until I get that first gulp of sugary goodness. After a few sips I usually feel like I've been hit over the head, so I wanted to soften the blow when I translated this love into cocktail form. This drink uses cola extract in place of its soda counterpart, so the final product has all the flavors of that nostalgic sip but in its purest form and minus the headache. I also opted not to top this cocktail with seltzer and instead gave it a rich texture by way of fresh pineapple juice.

TELL ME MORE

Singani is a Bolivian grape brandy and is considered the country's national liquor. It's beautifully floral with hints of muskmelon, and for me, it conjures up images of butterflies fluttering through the Andes mountains.

Party City

Best enjoyed when . . . *confetti is falling from the sky*

There is a very ill-named cocktail called the Mexican Firing Squad. While the name leaves much to be desired, the actual drink is outrageously tasty. I love this drink so much that we served it at our wedding. And let me tell you, we had a dance party of such epic proportions that I'm amazed no one fainted in the August heat of New York City. It was a sweaty lovefest, and I was grateful my wedding dress was short and backless. But for many of the party revelers, the day that followed was a hangover of epic proportions. So now, years later, this is my "thank you and sorry" to all my wedding guests—a truly chuggable version of its boozy predecessor.

Serves 1
Glassware: Highball
Ice: Cubed
Garnish: Lime wedge

1½ ounces Neversink Apple Apéritif

¾ ounce fresh lemon juice

½ ounce Jalapeño Blanco Tequila (page 258)

½ ounce Pomegranate Grenadine (page 252)

3 dashes Angostura bitters

Bubbly water, to top

Combine the Neversink, lemon juice, Jalapeño Blanco Tequila, pomegranate grenadine, and Angostura bitters in a shaker. Add ice and shake. Strain into a highball glass with cubed ice. Top with the bubbly water. Stir to incorporate all ingredients. Garnish with a lime wedge. Serve with a straw.

TELL ME MORE

Why do I call for Neversink Apple Apéritif? This drink will be pretty tasty with a traditional bottle of pommeau, but I love this specific apple mistelle because of its texture, which gives this cocktail real oomph.

Bamboozicle

Best enjoyed when . . . *your day is just not going as planned*

Like I've mentioned before, I'm always on a quest to spread the sherry love. As a loyal fan of the classic Bamboo cocktail (we had an adapted version of it on draft at Nitecap since day one), I wanted to present the drink in a less serious format while still maintaining and honoring its core recipe. Enter my brilliant husband, Jeremy, who some consider the slushy king. He said, "Wouldn't it be funny if you turned the Bamboo into a slushy?" I indeed thought it was a hilarious idea (bartenders have a weird sense of humor). In transforming the Bamboo, I was inspired by a trio of iconic blended cocktails—the Piña Colada, Margarita, and fruit Daiquiri. While this drink is most certainly perfect for an extra-hot day, it is also transportive during those long snowy winters.

Serves 1

Glassware: Double rocks

Ice: None

Garnish: Paper parasol, edible flower, and disco dust

1½ ounces amontillado sherry

1 ounce Simple Syrup (page 252)

¾ ounce white vermouth

¾ ounce dry vermouth

¾ ounce fresh orange juice

½ ounce strawberry puree

¼ ounce banana rum

Combine the sherry, syrup, white vermouth, dry vermouth, orange juice, strawberry puree, and banana rum in a blender with ½ cup of crushed ice. Blend on high for 15 to 20 seconds and pour into a double rocks glass. Garnish with paper parasol, edible flower, and disco dust. Serve with a straw but make sure it's not metal to avoid a lip-stuck-to-straw disaster!

Hack: If you can't find strawberry puree, use 2 whole strawberries, fresh or frozen, with an extra ¼ ounce simple syrup in its place.

TELL ME MORE

You might be wondering why the simple syrup content in this drink is so high. Blending something with ice mellows out flavors, and sugar amplifies them. If you turn a recipe not designed for a blender into a slushy, always increase your sugar content or you'll end up with bland frozen water.

Day Trip

Best enjoyed when . . . *did somebody say Patio Cocktail?!*

The simple yet enchanting mixture of lemonade and beer is one I've been sipping on for years. It's a fantastic way to elongate the already low-ABV beer into a truly sessionable beverage best accompanied by a burger and fries. It is no secret that the mixture of hops and citrus makes for a delightful pairing. Although this combination originally hails from Germany, I opted for a Belgian-style wheat beer to get that extra dose of hazy lemon. This cocktail is best enjoyed when served cold cold *cold*, so it should be drunk efficiently and refilled on the regular.

Serves 1
Glassware: Highball
Ice: None
Garnish: Lime wedge

1½ ounces Aperitivo Cappelletti

¾ ounce fresh lime juice

½ ounce Pineapple Gum Syrup (page 256)

¼ ounce Giffard Fruit de la Passion Liqueur

Belgian-style wheat beer, to top

Combine the Cappelletti, lime juice, pineapple gum syrup, and passion fruit liqueur in a shaker. Add ice and shake. Strain into a highball glass with no ice and top with the Belgian wheat beer. Garnish with a lime wedge.

TELL ME MORE

Don't forget to use up that bottle of Cappelletti in a spritz or highball.

Sweet Nothings

Best enjoyed when . . . *plotting to make someone fall head over heels for you*

The Pimm's Cup—a refreshing cooler traditionally served with citrus, fresh fruit, and ginger ale—is as delightful as it sounds. But it's also a little prim and proper and flesh-colored pantyhose-y. It's what aristocrats drink while watching a tennis match or taking evening strolls in their perfectly manicured gardens while their children play with the nanny, all wearing matching outfits. I mean, that's lovely and all, but I'm already yawning. So this version is a little grittier. In place of sugary ginger ale, we use a syrup made from fresh ginger, making it earthy, spicy, and deep. I've added a spoonful of blueberry preserves to coat your mouth and linger gloriously. Bubbles take form in Lambrusco, and I urge you to seek out a dry one, maybe even natural, to give it an added layer of funky vibez.

Serves 1

Glassware: Highball

Glass: Cubed

Garnish: Lemon wheel, mint bouquet, and fresh blueberries

1 ounce Contratto Aperitif

¾ ounce fresh lemon juice

½ ounce sloe gin

½ ounce Ginger Syrup (page 254)

1 tablespoon blueberry preserves (preferably Bonne Maman)

Dry Lambrusco wine, to top

Combine the Contratto Aperitif, lemon juice, sloe gin, ginger syrup, and blueberry preserves in a shaker. Add ice and shake. Fine-strain into a highball glass over cubed ice. Top with Lambrusco. Stir to incorporate all ingredients. Garnish with a lemon wheel, mint bouquet, and fresh blueberries. Serve with a straw.

TELL ME MORE

I specifically call for Bonne Maman blueberry preserves because they have the texture of pie filling—so yum in this cocktail!

Words of Wisdom

Best enjoyed when . . . *running your hands through someone's hair*

This highball is all about comfort and nostalgia. While sage is said to ward off evil spirits, it also has an immediate calming effect on me (perhaps because it wards off evil spirits). On the nose, it always reminds me of eucalyptus with a spritz of fresh lemon oil, warm and inviting, while also having an unexpected edge, a rawness. It's sort of like a rugged mountain man with a sensitive side. To calm the slight bitterness in the sage, I chose honey, and the combination creates a wonderful, almost fuzzy sensation on the tongue. That, along with the bubbles from the tonic water, make this serious-on-paper cocktail much more youthful.

Serves 1

Glassware: Wineglass

Ice: Cubed

Garnish: Lemon wheel and dried bay leaf

2 ounces Sage White Wine (page 258)

¼ ounce Honey Syrup (page 253)

½ teaspoon apricot liqueur

2 dashes Miracle Mile Bay Rum Bitters

Tonic water, to top

Combine the sage-infused white wine, syrup, apricot liqueur, and bitters in a wineglass with 3 hand-cracked ice cubes. Add more ice. Top with tonic water. Stir to chill and incorporate all ingredients. Garnish with a lemon wheel and dried bay leaf.

Green and Chill

Best enjoyed when . . . *eating a heaping plate of chilaquiles*

Celery is a truly an underappreciated vegetable. It gets painstakingly chopped into fine delicate pieces by cooks to be braised and sautéed with little regard from the eater, who just cares about the short rib. It's the vegetable left sitting lonely on the crudités platter; the garnish that gets violently ripped out of the Bloody Mary, abandoned on the table at the end of the meal along with the dirty napkins and check presenter. So I implore you, go get yourself a celery stick, break it in half, and take a good, deep whiff of its inviting, cooling, and crisp smell. Now take a bite. There's that initial satisfying crunch, which is quickly followed by a wave of vegetal yet sweet water. It's truly a glorious vegetable bursting with flavor, and this cocktail celebrates it. And please, don't forget the garnish on this one! It's there for a reason. . . .

Serves 1
Glassware: Highball
Ice: Cubed
Garnish: Celery ribbon

1½ ounces White Floc de Gascogne

¾ ounce fresh lime juice

½ ounce St. Germain elderflower liqueur

½ ounce Celery Syrup (page 257)

Bubbly water, to top

Combine the Floc de Gascogne, lime juice, St. Germain, and syrup in a shaker. Add ice and shake. Strain into a highball glass over cubed ice. Top with the bubbly water. Stir to incorporate all ingredients. Garnish with a celery ribbon. Serve with a straw.

TELL ME MORE

To get that perfect celery ribbon, use a peeler. Then place your ribbon in an ice-water bath to create a natural dainty curl.

Dancing Queen

Best enjoyed when . . . *realizing what a sophisticated adult you've become*

Amaretto has an undeserved bad reputation. Once mixed into an Amaretto Sour, it's the cocktail of choice of sorority houses. And honestly that's not even a sting against sorority houses, but aimed at the makers of sour mix from a soda gun, which causes this drink to become a sugary, mouth-numbing hangover from hell. I, like many other people, swore off this drink, until one day, the Goddess of Balance showed me the way. Fresh juice from an actual lemon replaced sour mix and was properly balanced with not only the simple syrup but the inherently sugary amaretto. I guess you could say I've rekindled my romance with this massively misunderstood liqueur.

Serves 1

Glassware: Coupe

Ice: None

Garnish: Expressed then discarded lemon twist and Angostura bitters swirl

1½ ounces Vermouth Limoncello (page 260)

1 ounce fresh lemon juice

½ ounce amaretto (preferably Caffo)

½ ounce Simple Syrup (page 252)

1 dash absinthe

1 organic egg white

Combine the vermouth limoncello, lemon juice, amaretto, syrup, absinthe, and egg white in a shaker. Pre-shake without ice. Add ice and shake. Fine-strain into a coupe glass. Express a lemon twist over cocktail then discard. Garnish with a swirl of Angostura bitters.

TELL ME MORE

Did you know that egg whites not only add a textural component, they also "mute" flavors? One way I kept this cocktail from tasting too sweet was by adding the egg white. So, if you are not an egg white fan, all good, but please don't make this drink without one as it will completely throw off the balance we tried so hard to achieve.

En Vogue

Best enjoyed when . . . *sporting a straw hat*

Cocktails with red wine are often related back to sangría. It's a very democratic cocktail, shared among friends with different likes and dislikes, poured out of a communal pitcher, often enjoyed during a family-style meal. It's an *easy* cocktail, almost too easy. So, well, I wanted to complicate things a bit and stir sh*t up. Hello, green Chartreuse! The recipe calls for only a quarter ounce of this pungent, wild herbal liqueur that dates back centuries, but boy, does it make an impact. When combined with rich, dark crème de cassis, you'll kind of feel like you are getting away with something, and let me tell you, it feels good.

Serves 1
Glassware: Wineglass
Ice: Cubed
Garnish: Brandied cherries

2 ounces full-bodied red wine

½ ounce fresh lemon juice

½ ounce crème de cassis

½ ounce Simple Syrup (page 252)

¼ ounce green Chartreuse

Combine the red wine, lemon juice, crème de cassis, syrup, and Chartreuse in a shaker. Add ice and give it a short shake. Strain into a wineglass over cubed ice. Garnish with brandied cherries.

Friendship Bracelet

Best enjoyed when . . . *petting a long-haired Persian cat*

This cocktail is inspired by my dear friend Lauren Corriveau, who was once my right-hand wing-woman at Nitecap. Additionally, Lauren might like French fries more than I do. There have been times when Lauren and I visited multiple bars in one night and ordered French fries at each along the way, for comparison's sake, you know. Research. Lauren has this ability to take flavors that I personally think sound pretty muddy together and magically turn them into the most delicious drinks ever. I think it's one of her many superpowers. One such flavor combination was a cocktail with red bell pepper juice and raspberry. In my mind it sounded terrible! But I would pretty much follow Lauren into a burning building, so I took a tiny sip, followed by another sip, followed by another. I couldn't put it down. It was so unbelievably good! This is an homage of sorts, with a double dose of raspberry taking the form of a syrup and a preserve.

Serves 1
Glassware: Double rocks
Ice: Large format
Garnish: 3 speared raspberries

1½ ounces H&H Rainwater Madeira

¾ ounce fresh lemon juice

¾ ounce fresh red bell pepper juice

½ ounce Martini & Rossi Fiero

½ ounce Raspberry Syrup (page 255)

1 heaping bar spoon of raspberry preserves

Combine the madeira, lemon juice, red bell pepper juice, Martini & Rossi Fiero, syrup, and raspberry preserves in a shaker. Add ice and shake. Fine-strain into a double rocks glass over large-format ice. Garnish with 3 raspberries on a pick.

TELL ME MORE

Martini & Rossi Fiero is a bittersweet aperitivo made with sweet Spanish oranges. If you could imagine what the color orange tastes like, this would be it. Round and carroty, it's perfect served with a splash of tonic and a hint of fresh citrus.

Dance Anthem

Best enjoyed when . . . *reminiscing about that foam party you attended when you were sixteen*

There are a lot of strong players in this drink, and at first glance I get that it might seem a little overwhelming. But surprisingly, this drink is a pretty easygoing, vegetal refresher. It kind of hits your body in the way biting into a Popsicle does, and you feel it all the way from your toes to your head. Pastis has this incredible cooling effect that sort of takes you out of your body. Cachaça, usually a free spirit, plays an uncharacteristic role in this formula as the grounding force. Together they lift the bright green, clean, crisp notes of the bell pepper. Lime peel is intensely fragrant, so by adding it directly to your drink, you infuse an entire dimension of flavor. You get texture, bitterness, and an almost piney quality that complements the pastis—like glitter on the dance floor.

Serves 1
Glassware: Double rocks
Ice: Cubed
Garnish: Lime wedge

4 juicy lime wedges

1 ounce Carpano Bianco vermouth

1 ounce Green Bell Pepper Syrup (page 254)

½ ounce pastis

½ ounce unaged cachaça

At the bottom of a shaker, muddle the 4 lime wedges. Add the Carpano Bianco, green bell pepper syrup, pastis, and cachaça. Add ice and shake vigorously. Pour the contents of the shaker into a double rocks glass. Top with more ice if needed. Garnish with a lime wedge. Serve with a straw.

State of Mind

Oh, Thai basil, how I love thee! Unlike Genovese basil, also known as Italian basil, the Thai variety has notes of anise and even a slight bit of spice. I was first introduced to Thai basil–infused blanc vermouth while working behind the bar at Mayahuel, an agave mecca. Already an avid fan of blanc vermouth (it's my go-to in a simple one-and-one highball), the addition of this fragrant and savory herb blew me away. Its presence was undeniable, and even though it has intense flavors, it didn't take away from all the delicate floral notes in the vermouth. In fact, it seemed to enhance them. This cocktail is dry, vegetal, and overwhelmingly thirst quenching. Be prepared to drink more than one.

Serves 1

Glassware: Double rocks

Ice: Large format

Garnish: Salt rim and cucumber slice (seedless)

1 seedless cucumber slice

1 ounce fino sherry

1 ounce Thai Basil Blanc Vermouth (page 258)

¾ ounce fresh lime juice

½ ounce Salted Cane Syrup (page 252)

At the bottom of a shaker, lightly muddle the cucumber slice. Add the fino sherry, Thai basil–infused vermouth, lime juice, and syrup to the shaker. Add ice and shake. Fine-strain into a salt-rimmed double rocks glass over large-format ice. Garnish with a cucumber slice.

STOOP SIPPER

SPLISH SPLASH

Splish Splash

Best enjoyed when . . . *the sidewalk is blisteringly hot*

August in New York City. It's the muggiest, sweatiest, why-do-I-have-to-wear-clothes-to-work kind of hot. It's depressing, it's suffocating, and it feels like there is no relief . . . until . . . you walk past a fire hydrant propelling a cool shower of rain into the sky. As it hits your skin, you feel renewed, even if for just that brief moment. All at once there's a little hop and skip in your walk, and getting to your next appointment doesn't feel all that awful anymore. . . . This drink does all that.

Serves 1
Glassware: Highball
Ice: Cubed
Garnish: Shiso leaf

2 shiso leaves
3 ounces fresh watermelon juice
1½ ounces yuzu sake

At the bottom of a highball glass, lightly muddle 2 shiso leaves. Add cubed ice and pour in the watermelon juice and yuzu sake. Gently stir to combine. Garnish with a shiso leaf delicately tucked behind the ice. Serve with a straw.

Stoop Sipper

Best enjoyed when . . . *you've decided it's okay to be running ten minutes behind*

Never ever in my life have I thought about, ordered, or craved iced tea. Until I'm at someone's house and they offer it to me. Then I will accept the glass without much fanfare, take a sip, and exclaim, "Why on earth don't I drink this supremely delicious and refreshing beverage more often?" And then somehow another year passes without another iced tea. When I started conceptualizing this book, I wrote myself a reminder: *Iced tea is your friend*. So here it is. My slightly spiked, smoky, cherry pit, marzipan, peachy, cooler iced tea.

Serves 1
Glassware: Festive
Ice: Cubed
Garnish: 3 lemon wheels

4 ounces chilled oolong tea
2 ounces Maurin Quina
1 teaspoon peach liqueur

Combine the chilled oolong tea, Maurin Quina, and peach liqueur in a festive glass filled with cubed ice. Stir to chill and incorporate ingredients. Garnish with 3 lemon wheels. Serve with a straw.

High and Low

Best enjoyed when . . . *you magically wake up one day and declare, "I'm cooking brunch!"*

Originally hailing from a coffee shop named Koppi in Sweden, the Coffee and Tonic is a mixture of cold brew coffee and tonic water served over ice. It has amassed a loyal, if not almost cultlike, following in the US. I'll be honest, when I first heard of this combination, I may have gagged a little. But then I reminded myself to remain open-minded, and after finally trying one, yup, I agreed—it was simply delicious! One version I gleefully slurped was garnished with a Luxardo maraschino cherry, and it was that combination that inspired this cocktail. Honestly, this is one of my favorite recipes in this collection of many, and I'd love for you to just stop reading and make one for yourself, so please, don't let me stand in your way.

Serves 1
Glassware: Highball
Ice: Cubed
Garnish: Plum fan

1½ ounces umeshu
1 ounce cold brew coffee
½ ounce oloroso sherry
Tonic water, to top

Combine the umeshu, coffee, sherry, and tonic water in a highball glass filled with cubed ice. Stir to incorporate ingredients. Garnish with a plum fan. Serve with a straw.

High Tide

Best enjoyed when . . . *feeling full of fire and needing an uplifting reminder that life is beautiful*

One of my all-time favorite "tricks" is adding a teaspoon of peated scotch whiskey to tart and juicy cocktails. Few things make such a big impact in such a small package. It adds a completely unexpected layer of flavor without hijacking the rest of the ingredients. I always think of it as a sort of wink at the end of a story, a little secret between my closest inner circle and myself. Here, the small pour of scotch, or as I like to call it smoky honey juice, is accompanied by a minuscule pour of potent, lush, and almost candy-like peach liqueur, creating a combination so highbrow/lowbrow, I almost can't stand it. This cocktail is for my sister, Alma, who I feel like would read this list of ingredients and be tickled. So here is my almost, maybe kind of tropical, but not really, dry sherry refresher.

Serves 1

Glassware: Double rocks

Ice: Large format

Garnish: Lemon wheel and brandied cherry flag*

1½ ounces amontillado sherry

¾ ounce fresh lemon juice

½ ounce Pineau des Charantes

½ ounce Cinnamon Syrup (page 255)

¼ ounce peach liqueur

1 teaspoon peated scotch whiskey

Combine the sherry, lemon juice, Pineau des Charantes, syrup, peach liqueur, and scotch in shaker. Add ice and shake. Strain into a double rocks glass with large-format ice. Garnish with a lemon wheel and brandied cherry flag.

*How to Make a Cherry Flag: Take your called-for citrus wheel or crescent and envelop a brandy cherry with it by folding it over the cherry from both ends. Keep in place by threading a cocktail pick from one end to the other.

Forever Crush

Best enjoyed when . . . *you're cleaning out your parents' basement and find your prom photo*

Honestly, this cocktail is all about making you feel giddy. A double dose of tartness makes you scrunch your nose. And I can't really think of anything more delicious than pineapples soaked in all the roasty juices of mezcal. There's something about this combination that just oozes eternal youth, open roads, messy hair, ripped jeans (from being lived in, not from some designer slashing them open and charging you more), and a life without alarm clocks.

Serves 1

Glassware: Coupe

Ice: None

Garnish: None

1½ ounces Cocchi Americano Bianco

¾ ounce fresh lemon juice

½ ounce Pineapple Mezcal (page 259)

½ ounce Simple Syrup (page 252)

1 teaspoon mango vinegar

Combine the Cocchi Americano, lemon juice, pineapple-infused mezcal, syrup, and mango vinegar in a shaker. Add ice and shake. Fine-strain into a coupe glass.

Easy-Peasy One, Two, Three

SUZE AND ELDERFLOWER TONIC

Serves 1

Glassware: Highball

Ice: Cubed

Garnish: Lemon wedge

2 ounces Suze apéritif

4 ounces Fever Tree Elderflower Tonic Water

In a highball glass over cubed ice, build the Suze and elderflower tonic. Gently stir to incorporate. Garnish with a lemon wedge. Serve with a straw.

WINE AND PEACH

Serves 1

Glassware: Wineglass

Ice: Cubed

Garnish: Lemon twist

5 ounces Grüner Veltliner wine

1 teaspoon peach liqueur

In a wineglass over cubed ice, build the wine and peach liqueur. Gently stir to incorporate. Garnish with a lemon twist.

ROSÉ VERMOUTH AND SODA

Serves 1

Glassware: Highball

Ice: Cubed

Garnish: Lemon wheel and brandied cherries (as in plural!)

2 ounces Cola Lustau Rosé Vermut (page 258)

4 ounces Topo Chico sparkling mineral water

In a highball glass over cubed ice, build the Cola Rosé Vermouth and sparkling water. Gently stir to incorporate. Garnish with a lemon wheel and brandied cherries. Serve with a straw.

BEER AND BITTER

Serves 1

Glassware: Highball

Ice: None

Garnish: Orange slice

9 ounces Belgian-style wheat beer

1 ounce red bitter of your choice (see page 67), chilled

In a highball glass, combine the beer and red bitter. Garnish with an orange slice. Try not to finish in two sips.

SUZE AND
ELDERFLOWER TONIC

WINE AND
PEACH

ROSÉ VERMOUTH
AND SODA

BEER AND
BITTER

Prepare to be transported to a world where soft pajama sets, cashmere socks, and fancy linen sheets are the norm. In this world, the coffee is always the right temperature, the French fry in your hand has a perfect golden crisp, the eggs are jammy, and somehow you always end up back on your chaise lounge with a cocktail in your hand. Listen, I don't even own a chaise lounge, but a girl can dream! The cocktails in this sections don't contain any fruit juice, so give your arm a rest, grab a mixing glass, and start stirring. If you've ever wondered what a three-Martini lunch would look like minus the twenty ounces of chilled vodka, this is your moment to thrive. These drinks make you slow down, not in the "I just had one too many Old-Fashioned's, I can't walk so fast, please slow down" way, but in the "Ah, I want to live in this moment forever" kind of way. They make you ponder and reflect. Equally great for totally casual post–James Joyce book club hangouts or all-important debates about whether pineapple belongs on pizza. Cocktails to make you ponder, question, and feel engaged.

Soulful and Silky, Cocktails That Encourage Deep Thoughts but Keep You Wild at Heart

LANDSCAPE
PAINTING,
PAGE 143

CENTERFOLD,
PAGE 140

SAME DIFFERENCE,
PAGE 140

important: three, yes, precisely three, brandied cherries, to be delicately eaten, one by one, making sure to save one cherry for that perfect final sip.

Serves 1

Glassware: Nick and Nora

Ice: None

Garnish: 3 speared brandied cherries

2 ounces sweet vermouth (preferably Carpano Antica)

¾ ounce rye whiskey

¼ ounce unaged cherry brandy

½ teaspoon Branca Menta

1 dash absinthe

Combine the sweet vermouth, rye whiskey, cherry brandy, Branca Menta, and absinthe in a chilled mixing glass. Add ice and stir. Strain into a Nick and Nora glass. Garnish with 3 brandied cherries on a cocktail pick.

Landscape Painting

Best enjoyed when . . . *did somebody say, "Sweater weather"?!*

Spazieren is a German word that, like many German words, is very specific but doesn't quite have an English equivalent. *Spazieren* means to take a walk, but it's not just a walk, it's more of a stroll, one you take out of pure enjoyment and ideally in nature, like in a forest. I haven't been back to Germany in a long time to able to check ye old walk in the Black Forest off my bucket list yet, so in its place I made a cocktail inspired by what I imagine this walk would be like. And the garnish is

TELL ME MORE

Unaged cherry brandy, traditionally known as Kirschwasser, is a wildly underappreciated and misunderstood bottle of booze. No, it's not sweet! Quite the opposite. Delicious either on its own after a meal or poured over pistachio ice cream, don't let this bottle sit around on your back bar.

Centerfold

Best enjoyed when . . . *feeling like you want to rebel*

There is nothing traditional about this cocktail. Yes, it's somewhat reminiscent of a classic Martini, but even its barely pale green color suggests that you have signed yourself up for something a little out of the ordinary. The bright, crisp heat of a jalapeño is a natural friend of the almost musky and juicy mango, but throw in a flowering, earthy bouquet of alpine herbs, and you'll find yourself in a threesome you never knew you wanted or needed.

Serves 1
Glassware: Nick and Nora
Ice: None
Garnish: None

1½ ounces white vermouth
¾ ounce Jalapeño Blanco Tequila (page 258)
½ ounce génépi
1 teaspoon Rhine Hall mango brandy

Combine the white vermouth, jalapeño-infused tequila, génépi, and mango brandy in a chilled mixing glass. Add ice and stir. Strain into a Nick and Nora glass.

Same Difference

Best enjoyed when . . . *wanting to play the part of the seducer*

This cocktail is very clearly inspired by the formidable Negroni—a drink that I adore and have a hard time turning down. But the Negroni is not for the faint of heart (or for those who accidentally drink on an empty stomach), as it packs a punch. Here is my version that is meant to make you slow down and nonchalantly play footsie with your new flame.

Serves 1
Glassware: Double rocks
Ice: Large format
Garnish: Orange wheel

1½ ounces fino sherry
1 ounce Cocchi Americano Rosa
½ ounce Cacao Nib Campari (page 259)
1 heaping bar spoon of cherry preserves

Combine the fino sherry, Cocchi Rosa, cacao-infused Campari, and cherry preserves in a chilled mixing glass. Add ice and stir. Fine-strain into a double rocks glass over large-format ice. Garnish with an orange wheel.

Panda-Monium

Best enjoyed when . . . *feeling totally happy about being you*

There's nothing quite like a perfectly tailored monochrome pantsuit. It casts a striking silhouette in spite of its simplicity. Or maybe precisely because of its simplicity. And so, I will not try to complicate the intro to this cocktail and will instead let you unbutton your blazer and sip away.

Serves 1

Glassware: Nick and Nora

Ice: None

Garnish: Grapefruit twist, discarded

1½ ounces amontillado sherry

1½ ounces Cocchi Americano Rosa

1 dash orange bitters

1 dash grapefruit bitters

Combine the amontillado sherry, Cocchi Rosa, orange bitters, and grapefruit bitters in a mixing glass. Add ice and stir. Strain into a Nick and Nora glass. For a garnish, express a grapefruit twist into the glass and discard the peel.

Sin-A-Rama

Best enjoyed when . . . *you're being all serious but just want to party*

I call this a *segue cocktail*, a cocktail to bridge the gap between two different styles. It may sound crazy, but think of this drink as a sort of hybrid Martini Sour (did I just blow your mind!?). If you lean toward shaken refreshing drinks but want to dip your toes into the stirred cocktail world, this might be the gentle transition you are looking for. It's juicy yet rich. It's tart yet silky. The combination of pommeau and Cocchi Americano creates an apple flavor that's ripe and crunchy yet somehow caramelized and baked. Throw in a little tropical surprise by way of passion fruit and you've got yourself the perfect intro to a cocktail that makes you ponder and dig a little deeper.

Serves 1
Glassware: Nick and Nora
Ice: None
Garnish: Orange twist

- **1½ ounces pommeau**
- **1 ounce Cocchi Americano Bianco**
- **½ ounce white verjus**
- **1 teaspoon Giffard Fruit de la Passion Liqueur**
- **1 dash orange bitters**

Combine the pommeau, Cocchi Americano, verjus, passion fruit liqueur, and orange bitters in a chilled mixing glass. Add ice and stir. Strain into a Nick and Nora glass. Garnish with an expressed orange twist.

TELL ME MORE

Remember when I said that this chapter has no fruit juice in it? Well, I was kind of lying. Verjus is the unfermented pressed juice from unripe wine grapes. It's super high in acid, and flavor-wise it can be compared to vinegar. I often liken it to Granny Smith apple juice. I love using it in stirred cocktails that need brightness while still being able to maintain the smooth texture that makes a stirred cocktail so special.

RELUCTANT
STAR,
PAGE 145

STILL-LIFE,
PAGE 146

WISH LIST,
PAGE 146

Reluctant Star

Best enjoyed when . . . *physically tied to your computer but mentally taking a pie out of the oven*

If I were to suggest a food pairing in this book, it would be to accompany this cocktail with a scoop of rich, creamy vanilla ice cream. And I'm going to get a bit snobby for a second here. I'm not talking Breyer's. I'm talking decadent Tahitian vanilla ice cream. You know, the kind where you're in the ice cream aisle, staring at all your options, and one tub costs $2.99 while the other costs $8.99 and you're like, "But it's just vanilla ice cream. How much better can one be than the other?!" And have I told you all about my love of combining aged apple brandy with aquavit before? Because it's an important love that I feel in every limb of my body. When combined, they basically make a cookie. And if I haven't managed to sell you on this cocktail yet, even after mentioning pie, ice cream, and cookies, then I'm not sure if I'm qualified to endorse anything ever again.

Serves 1
Glassware: Single rocks
Ice: None
Garnish: Lemon twist, discarded

1½ ounces Pineau des Charantes
¾ ounce Cocchi Americano Bianco
½ ounce aged apple brandy
½ ounce aged aquavit (preferably Linie)
Absinthe, to rinse glass

Combine the Pineau des Charantes, Cocchi Americano, apple brandy, and aged aquavit in a chilled mixing glass. Add ice and stir. Strain into an absinthe-rinsed, chilled single rocks glass. For garnish, express a lemon twist into the glass and discard the peel.

Still-Life

Best enjoyed when . . . *ordering a second round of desserts*

What I love about an Old-Fashioned is that it transforms over time. Your first sip can almost take you by surprise. It's sharp. It's biting. But with each sip, you can see corners turning into rounded edges. When I started thinking about creating a low-ABV version of this iconic cocktail, I wanted it to take you on the same kind of journey. Imagine this cocktail as a conversation about a rather heated topic. There may be conflict at first, but by the end, there is some sort of resolution, a coming together. And hopefully the drink helped.

Serves 1
Glassware: Double rocks
Ice: Large format
Garnish: Orange twist

1 ounce H&H Rainwater Madeira
½ ounce Amaro Nonino
¼ ounce Grand Marnier
¼ ounce grappa
½ teaspoon Salted Cane Syrup (page 252)

Combine the madeira, Amaro Nonino, Grand Marnier, grappa, and syrup in a mixing glass. Add ice and stir. Strain into a double rocks glass over large-format ice. Garnish with an orange twist.

Wish List

Best enjoyed when . . . *you're too lazy to pick up the confetti*

This oddball of a highball should be sipped in the same manner as one would a Manhattan—slowly, pondering the meaning of something big. Since this drink has soda pop in it, that something big can certainly be whether or not Jen and Brad had the best couples style ever (remember their effortless matching cargo pants phase?!).

Serves 1
Glassware: Highball
Ice: Cubed
Garnish: Lime wheel and orange crescent

2 ounces Punt e Mes
¼ ounce Amaro Meletti
¼ ounce amaretto (preferably Caffo)
2 dashes Miracle Mile Chocolate Chili Bitters
Cane cola, to top

In a highball glass filled with cubed ice, combine the Punt e Mes, Amaro Meletti, amaretto, chocolate chili bitters, and cola. Stir to combine. Garnish with a lime wheel and orange crescent. Serve with a straw.

TELL ME MORE

Punt e Mes is a delight in a simple one-and-one highball and can also make for an interesting Manhattan.

puffing stick with this beverage. I'd also like to point out that this is one of those drinks where glassware makes an impact. The double rocks glass you choose for this should ideally have a heavy base, perhaps made of (faux) crystal, and feel sturdy. Basically, you'll instantly become *very* important.

Serves 1
Glassware: Double rocks
Ice: Large format
Garnish: Orange twist

1 ounce oloroso sherry

¾ ounce amber vermouth

½ ounce Pedro Ximénez sherry

½ ounce cognac

1 teaspoon coffee liqueur

Combine the oloroso sherry, amber vermouth, Pedro Ximénez sherry, cognac, and coffee liqueur in a chilled mixing glass. Add ice and stir. Strain into a double rocks glass over large-format ice. Garnish with an orange twist.

Important People

Best enjoyed when . . . *rewarding yourself with an extra hour of luxurious free time*

Out of all of the cocktails in this book, I'd say that this is the most *serious*. Maybe that's just because we all have this preconceived notion that Cognac is very fancy-pants, which, yeah, okay, it is, but fancy shouldn't mean inaccessible. This recipe calls for a tiny measure of that good stuff, which gives the sherry and vermouth that extra va-va-voom factor. I'm not a cigar smoking kind of girl, but if I were, I would, with 100 percent certainty, pair my mighty

TELL ME MORE

Okay, so earlier I said there were four types of vermouth. I'm here to tell you about another, a fifth, less-known variety. Amber, or ambrato vermouth, tastes to me as if someone took a dry vermouth and added a soft touch of honey to the bottle. I love sipping on it in a highball with some dry tonic and a squeeze of lemon.

Fair Play

Best enjoyed when . . . *frolicking in the French countryside among fields of fresh lavender*

When it comes to culinary achievements, the French are venerable hitmakers! Who can turn down a steaming bowl of *moules frites*? A perfectly flaky, indulgently buttery croissant? A crisp, cascading glass of Champagne? Not I! Wine—they've got it! Cognac—yup! But we don't often think of the French when it comes to bitter liqueurs, and that, my friends, is where we've all taken a giant misstep. Enter my bestie, Suze. Yes, bitter, but also floral, savory, piney, and an all-around delight of an apéritif. Now combine that with Lillet Blanc and you've got yourself a vanilla- and orange-scented cloud of happiness.

Serves 1
Glassware: Double rocks
Ice: Large format
Garnish: Orange wheel

1½ ounces Lillet Blanc
½ ounce Suze apéritif
½ ounce dry vermouth (preferably Mulassano Extra Dry)
½ ounce bourbon
1 heaping bar spoon of orange marmalade

Combine the Lillet Blanc, Suze, dry vermouth, bourbon, and orange marmalade in a chilled mixing glass. Add ice and stir. Fine-strain into a double rocks glass with large-format ice. Garnish with an orange wheel.

TELL ME MORE

I opted for Mulassano Extra Dry Vermouth in this drink because of its distinctive bouquet of tarragon and lemon balm that I think plays gorgeously with the Suze.

EASY ACCESS

GOLDEN FANTASY

Easy Access

Best enjoyed when . . . *wearing crimson velvet*

I'm not gonna lie, this cocktail is a strange bird. I guess, when you think about it, peacocks are pretty strange birds, but who doesn't appreciate a good peacock sighting? While I would never dare compare a cocktail creation to the spectacular workings of Mother Nature, I find this unusual combination of ingredients a delightful surprise. If a holiday cinnamon cookie got a tropical twist and was topped with celebratory bubbles, this would be the result.

Serves 1
Glassware: Coupe
Ice: None
Garnish: None

1 ounce Lillet Rouge

½ ounce Jamaican rum

¼ ounce crème de cacao

¼ ounce coconut liqueur (preferably Kalani)

¼ ounce banana liqueur (preferably Giffard)

Dry sparkling white wine, to top

Combine the Lillet Rouge, rum, crème de cacao, coconut liqueur, and banana liqueur in a chilled mixing glass. Add ice and stir. Strain into a coupe glass. Top with sparkling wine.

Golden Fantasy

Best enjoyed when . . . *the world feels all too overwhelming*

I'm usually pretty willing to let people substitute ingredients if they can't find what's called for, but I'm going to be very strict here—if you can't get your hands on a bottle of brandy made from mirabelle plums, then PLEASE do not make this cocktail. I know it might sound absolutely absurd to have an entire experience hinge on a teaspoon of plum brandy, but that is precisely what I'm saying. My ego thanks you in advance.

Serves 1
Glassware: Nick and Nora
Ice: None
Garnish: None

2½ ounces umeshu

½ ounce Japanese whiskey

1 teaspoon mirabelle plum brandy

2 dashes cherry bitters

Combine the umeshu, Japanese whiskey, mirabelle plum brandy, and cherry bitters in a chilled mixing glass. Add ice and stir. Strain into a Nick and Nora glass.

Love Language

Best enjoyed when . . . *reclining, arms stretched high, toes curled*

Can you think of anything more delectable, more joyous, or more satisfying than a fresh, perfectly ripe, juicy, fragrant tomato?! Nor can I! To me, tomato season officially means summer. And summer means dips in the lake, a rotation of vegetables on the grill, and the never-ending, relentless search for the perfect dress that is simultaneously flattering and bag-like. When I think Martini, however, I don't immediately think "Yum, refreshing!" Well, you guessed it—I'm here to change your mind. The key to this cocktail is making sure that it is colder than cold. I recommend that your sherry, vermouth, and Lillet come straight from the fridge when mixing this recipe up, so if you're using unopened bottles, definitely chill them beforehand.

Serves 1
Glassware: Nick and Nora
Ice: None
Garnish: Tomolive*

1 ripe cherry tomato
1½ ounces Lillet Rosé
¾ ounce fino sherry
¾ ounce dry vermouth
1 teaspoon strawberry liqueur

At the bottom of your mixing glass, gently muddle the cherry tomato. Add the Lillet Rosé, fino sherry, dry vermouth, and strawberry liqueur. Add ice and stir. Fine-strain into a Nick and Nora glass. Garnish with a tomolive.

*Tomolives are bright and briny pickled green tomatoes. Best served cold!

Press Pause

Best enjoyed when . . . *fresh out of a steaming hot bath*

This is my ode to the Pisco Sour. And yes, I am aware that this cocktail does not have (1) pisco, (2) citrus, or (3) egg white, all defining factors of the Pisco Sour . . . but I swear, it is indeed inspired by a Pisco Sour. In place of pisco, I've enlisted the forces of what shall here on out be known as the Grapey Triumvirate: Floc de Gascogne, Singani, and grappa. I find that both Pisco and FDG have these totally wild floral notes, while Singani is like diving into a bouquet of blossoming pink roses. The grappa, on the other hand, is a bit more rugged and gives the drink a little edge. It's fascinating to compare three entirely different spirits, from opposite sides of the world, all made from the same raw material, and see how they can complement and extract new flavors from each other. While you will most certainly need to activate your imagination to experience this parallel Pisco Sour universe, it is precisely imagination that we adults could use more of in our daily lives.

Serves 1

Glassware: Nick and Nora

Ice: None

Garnish: Lime twist

2½ ounces white Floc de Gascogne

½ ounce Singani (preferably Singani 63)

1 teaspoon Clear Creek Pinot Grigio Grappa

1 drop eucalyptus extract

Combine the Floc de Gascogne, Singani, grappa, and eucalyptus extract in a chilled mixing glass. Add ice and stir. Strain into a Nick and Nora glass. Garnish with an expressed lime twist.

Promise Julep

Best enjoyed when ... *you undo the top button of your jeans*

You've had an intense day at work, followed by a crowded commute home. The shoes you've been wearing all day have left your toes cramped and your back aching. YOU JUST WANT PIZZA FROM THAT ONE PLACE, but it's Monday and they are closed Mondays, which you didn't know, so you fantasized about their pizza all throughout your dreadful day and were counting on said pizza as the reward to get you through it all. You are supremely disappointed but then remember you have a mediocre frozen pizza that you can heat up. You go ahead and do that because sometimes we must settle, but your body is still filled with rage. Because you are a problem solver and an overachiever, you think of the perfect task to calm your nerves. You grab a ziplock bag, fill it with ice, take hold of a hammer, and start banging away. Ta-da, you have crushed ice. You add some booze and after one sip, you remember that most problems are solved by liquids on crushed ice. Your pizza is ready and it's the most delicious pizza you've ever eaten. You didn't want to deal with that oversize pizza box anyway.

Serves 1
Glassware: Julep tin
Ice: Crushed
Garnish: Lavish mint bouquet

5 or 6 mint leaves
2 ounces pommeau
½ ounce Irish whiskey
½ teaspoon Demerara Syrup (page 252)
1 dash cardamom bitters

Rub the mint leaves around the inside of the glass. Discard the mint. Add the pommeau, Irish whiskey, syrup, and cardamom bitters to the glass. Fill halfway with crushed ice and swizzle. Top with more crushed ice and snow-cone it (see Speaking of Crushed Ice, page 77). Garnish with a lavish mint bouquet. Serve with a straw.

Quick little warning: Cardamom bitters are INTENSE and can completely take over a drink. So please make sure to truly stick to one single dash in this recipe.

TELL ME MORE

Many people leave their muddled mint at the bottom of the glass. But I find that mint, and some other herbs as well, start becoming bitter the longer it sits submerged under ice and liquid or when being violently stabbed by a straw over and over again. The flavor we are trying to capture for our cocktails from mint lies in its oils, which can be extracted and infused into the drink with a light muddle, a quick shake, or a rubdown à la this julep recipe.

Summer Feelings

Best enjoyed when . . . *wanting to live in a glitter-dusted fairy wonderland*

This cocktail reminds me of lace. And I'm not talking about some lace doily your relative has framed in their kitchen. I'm talking couture runway lace. It's delicate. It's intricate. It's glamorous. Made even more gorgeous by a sparkly embellishment here and there. The ingredients combined here are like soft whispers, punctuated by different botanicals, each patiently waiting its turn to reveal itself. But honestly, all poetry aside, this drink is just super fun, full of surprises, and very pretty to look at.

Serves 1
Glassware: Double rocks
Ice: Large format
Garnish: Lemon wheel

2½ ounces white vermouth
½ ounce pisco
1 teaspoon Forthave Spirits Red Aperitivo
½ teaspoon crème de violette liqueur

Combine the white vermouth, pisco, Forthave Red, and crème de violette in a mixing glass. Add ice and stir. Strain into a double rocks glass with large-format ice. Garnish with a lemon wheel.

Adore You

Best enjoyed when . . . *savoring a three-course lunch*

Listen, as a bartender that makes fancy-schmancy cocktails, I'm not supposed to love a good old Dirty Martini. But I do and have zero shame about it, and neither should you. Honestly, what is better than a Martini and a salt lick all in one devilish liquid package? But I am supposed to make fancy-schmancy drinks (and since I just can't help myself), I've "done it up" a bit. Without the texture of gin or vodka, I opted for Cocchi Americano. While slightly bitter, there is no denying that Cocchi Americano also introduces some fruity notes, so to balance those out and truly adhere to the essence of this savory classic, a quick toasted-caraway infusion keeps this drink in the earthy realm where it deserves to be.

Serves 1

Glassware: V-Martini

Ice: None

Garnish: 3 speared olives

2 ounces dry vermouth

¾ ounce Caraway Cocchi Americano Bianco (page 257)

¼ ounce olive brine

Combine the vermouth, caraway-infused Cocchi Americano, and olive brine in a chilled mixing glass. Add ice and stir. Strain into a V-Martini glass. Garnish with 3 olives on a pick.

TELL ME MORE

Since this cocktail has some fruit notes to it, I highly recommend not using an overly salty brine here. I opted for green Castelvetrano olive brine when conceiving this recipe—it's on the lighter side, not murky and muddy like some other olive brines can be.

Easy-Peasy One, Two, Three

SHERRY AND VERMOUTH

Serves 1

Glassware: Double rocks

Ice: Large format

Garnish: Lemon and orange twists

2 ounces amontillado sherry

2 ounces white vermouth

In a double rocks glass with large-format ice, build the sherry and vermouth. Stir to incorporate and chill all ingredients. Garnish with expressed lemon and orange twists.

PORT AND AMARO

Serves 1

Glassware: Double rocks

Ice: Large format

Garnish: Orange twist

2 ounces white port

¼ ounce Forthave Spirits Marseille Amaro

In a double rocks glass with large-format ice, build the white port and amaro. Stir to incorporate and chill all ingredients. Garnish with an expressed orange twist.

APPLE AND PDC

Serves 1

Glassware: Single rocks

Ice: Crushed

Garnish: Lavish mint bouquet

2 ounces Neversink Apple Apéritif

½ ounce Pineau des Charantes

Combine the Neversink and Pineau des Charantes in a single rocks glass. Fill halfway with crushed ice and swizzle. Top with more crushed ice and snow-cone it (see Speaking of Crushed Ice, page 77). Garnish with a lavish mint bouquet. Serve with a straw.

APPLE
AND PDC

SHERRY AND
VERMOUTH

PORT AND
AMARO

DECADENT TREATS

This chapter is all about embracing your soul's undeniable need for over-the-top declarations of love. Don't fight it. This chapter is also about how deserving your soul is of those over-the-top declarations of love. Some of these cocktails might seem a little like dessert, and that's the point. Think cocktails with a touch of coconut milk, fortified ice cream floats, and just some all-around delicious and comforting treats. Because who are we kidding, we always have room for dessert—that's why we have a regular stomach and a dessert stomach, duh! Perhaps you've just feasted on a vibrant meal and need a change of pace. Perhaps it's Tuesday at 4 p.m. and a creamy cocktail just sounds really delicious in that moment. Perhaps you want to present someone a love song in cocktail form. Whatever scenario you may find yourself in, is there really ever a bad time for a little liquid prize?!

*Lush,
Indulgent, and
Gratifying, Drinks
to Reward Yourself
and Give In To*

Blank Space

Best enjoyed when . . . *nostalgia hits you hard*

Growing up, we didn't go out to restaurants or cafés much. My mother saved money every way she could, so eating out when we could just "make something even better at home," as she liked to say, seemed like a frivolity. Of course, everyone, including my mom, needs the occasional meal out, even if it's just to break the monotony of doing dishes every night, so every now and then my mother and I would venture to the Indian restaurant down the street. It was a special occasion made even more special by the addition of their mango lassi. I knew that my mom considered this part of the order completely superfluous but also acknowledged what a treat it was for me, and thus it went against her rational mind and gave in to just being in the moment.

Serves 1

Glassware: Highball

Ice: Crushed

Garnish: Pistachio nut crumble* and lemon zest

1½ ounces amontillado sherry

1½ ounces Mango-Honey Syrup (page 253)

½ ounce Moscatel sherry

½ ounce organic heavy cream

¼ ounce fresh lemon juice

Combine the amontillado sherry, syrup, Moscatel sherry, heavy cream, and lemon juice in a shaker. Add ice and shake. Strain into a highball glass over crushed ice. Garnish with pistachio nut crumble and lemon zest. Serve with a straw.

* What is pistachio nut crumble? Perhaps I made it sound fancier than it actually is, because it's literally just finely chopped pistachio nuts.

ONE UP,
PAGE 169

CLASS ACT,
PAGE 170

HIGHBALL TO
HEAVEN,
PAGE 170

One Up

Best enjoyed when . . . *needing order and calm*

Many folks misconstrue white créme de cacao and that's a shame because it is SO GOOD. I think when most people read "crème de cacao" on a cocktail menu, they immediately think the cocktail will be cloyingly sweet. Well people, with all due respect, we aren't making giant chocolate martinis served in garish glasses with some sort of absurd crumbled candy cane rim here. So please, rid yourself of your preconceived prejudices against this perfectly wonderful liqueur and you'll open yourself up to a whole other dimension of mouth treats.

Serves 1

Glassware: Nick and Nora

Ice: None

Garnish: Fennel pollen, optional*

¾ ounce amontillado sherry

¾ ounce white crème de cacao

¾ ounce fennel liqueur

¾ ounce organic heavy cream

Combine the amontillado sherry, white crème de cacao, fennel liqueur, and heavy cream in a shaker. Add ice and shake. Fine-strain into a Nick and Nora glass. Garnish with optional fennel pollen dusting.

* I say "optional" because fennel pollen is very expensive. Harvesting it is incredibly labor intensive. If you feel like splurging, please do, as it adds an incredible savory note to the cocktail. If you'd rather skip it, it's all good. I made this drink to taste delicious either way.

Class Act

Best enjoyed when . . . *celebrating that little victory*

Friends, this cocktail is simply about bringing you joy. No-nonsense, unapologetic joy. Because if fresh, frothy pineapple juice combined with spiced pears can't bring you joy, then I'm not sure anything can. It's the kind of drink I would enjoy if, say, someone wanted to surprise me with breakfast in bed (hint, hint), or as a way to elongate a perfectly spectacular day for just a few more blissful moments.

Serves 1
Glassware: Coupe
Ice: None
Garnish: Pineapple wedge

1 ounce Pineau des Charantes
¾ ounce fresh pineapple juice
½ ounce Singani (preferably Singani 63)
½ ounce spiced pear liqueur (preferably St. George)
½ ounce fresh lemon juice
½ ounce Simple Syrup (page 252)

Combine the Pineau des Charantes, pineapple juice, Singani, spiced pear liqueur, lemon juice, and syrup in a shaker. Add ice and shake. Fine-strain into a coupe and garnish with a pineapple wedge.

Highball to Heaven

Best enjoyed when . . . *you just need a hydrating hug*

After a busy day of running around, doing this and that, there is nothing quite as satisfying as fixing yourself a proper cocktail. I call this adulting. The second I enter my house, my pants fly off faster than you can say "clove-studded orange crescent," and I realign and recalibrate with this ultra-luxe highball that feels part sophisticated screen siren and part off-duty club kid.

Serves 1
Glassware: Highball
Ice: Crushed
Garnish: Clove-studded orange crescent

2 ounces Clove White Port (page 260)
1½ ounces Orange Cream Syrup (page 255)
1 dash Citric Acid Solution (page 261)
Bubbly water, to top

Combine the clove-infused port, syrup, and citric acid in a shaker. Whip shake. Pour all the contents into a highball glass over crushed ice. Top with bubbly water. Stir to incorporate all ingredients. Garnish with a clove-studded orange crescent. Serve with a straw.

In Her Glory

Best enjoyed when . . . *while sharing an over-the-top seafood platter*

Somehow nothing feels more extravagant than popping a bottle of bubbles open and gleefully pouring them over crushed ice. Perhaps it's because it feels a little like an act of rebellion. Something that might make a Champagne snob shudder in horror. You're doing what with that?! But you know better than to just conform, so why not make juleps with bubbly wine and why not combine an ingredient from South America with an ingredient from Japan? This rebel without a cause veers far from the original julep (which dates back to the 1800s), and the result is a cocktail that's both supremely floral and downright musky.

Serves 1

Glassware: Julep tin

Ice: Crushed

Garnish: Lavish mint bouquet and matcha powder

5 or 6 mint leaves

3 ounces dry white sparkling wine

½ ounce Singani (preferably Singani 63)

¼ ounce St. Germain elderflower liqueur

1 teaspoon Honey Syrup (page 253)

2 dashes matcha bitters

Rub the mint leaves around the inside of the cup. Discard the mint. Add the sparkling wine, Singani, St. Germain, syrup, and matcha bitters to the glass. Fill the glass halfway with crushed ice and swizzle. Top with more crushed ice and snow-cone it (see Speaking of Crushed Ice, page 77). Garnish with a lavish mint bouquet and a dusting of matcha powder. Serve with a straw.

TELL ME MORE

I use Cecil & Merl Matcha Bitters, which are infused with jasmine tea and peach. Oh my!

Flip the Script

Best enjoyed when . . . *they run out of cake!*

In a past life, I was an actress. After college, my life revolved around auditioning. Many days were spent running from one audition to the next, back to back, for hours on end, leaving little time to eat. So, like any clear-thinking thespian, I would sometimes make a quick stop at a bar and drink a Guinness, because if you didn't know, Guinness basically counts as food, as it's rich in iron and very filling. After my fortifying liquid meal, I would continue on with my auditions. And now that I read this all back to myself, I can't help but think that perhaps this is why I never made it as an actress. Well, anyhow, here is my jazzed-up stout beer cocktail that somehow tastes like cake.

Serves 1

Glassware: Fizz

Ice: None

Garnish: Freshly grated nutmeg

2 ounces red Macvin du Jura

1 ounce barista-quality oat milk
    (preferably Oatly)

¼ ounce Demerara Syrup (page 252)

1 teaspoon St. Elizabeth Allspice Dram
    Liqueur

1 whole organic egg

Stout beer,
    to top

Combine the Macvin du Jura, oat milk, syrup, allspice liqueur, and egg in a shaker. Pre-shake without ice, making sure the whole egg is properly incorporated. Add ice and shake. Fine-strain into a fizz glass. Top with stout. Garnish with freshly grated nutmeg.

TELL ME MORE

Egg white adds that delicious frothy texture to a cocktail. A whole egg, on the other hand, adds an almost custardy feel to a drink, making it seem that much more decadent. Sign me up! One quick note about using whole eggs—besides, of course, making sure they're fresh and free-range and organic, if possible—is that they can mute flavors. Don't be surprised if you need to add more of another element than usual. Whole egg cocktails are also a great opportunity to use bottles of bold, loud booze without sucker-punching someone.

It's a Mood

Best enjoyed when . . . *wearing grubby, worn-out sweatpants sitting next to your dearest and nearest, exchanging secrets*

As a teenager, I would say, I was pretty good about keeping my cool in public. Sure, I had a crush on a certain member of the Backstreet Boys, but when I purchased, of course totally ironically, a ticket to see the Backstreet Boys at an arena that was three hours away, because I had a great sense of humor, it was just to have a fun night with my girlfriend. You know, because it was funny! Did totally cool and collected teenage Natasha who smoked cigarettes in between class hurl her body over a wall of screaming girls so that she could try to touch one of the Backstreet Boys as they passed by? Oh yes. Yes, she did. So, let me just say, the color of this cocktail is enough to send any human with even a slight detection of hormones into a complete frenzy. But don't worry, the flavors of this teenage dream are all grown up.

Serves 1

Glassware: Festive

Ice: Crushed

Garnish: Dried rose petals, coconut flakes, and fresh lemon zest

2 ounces Bruto Americano

1½ ounces fresh pineapple juice

1½ ounces Coconut Mix (page 253)

¼ ounce fresh lemon juice

1 teaspoon rose liqueur

3 dashes Peychaud bitters

Combine the Bruto Americano, pineapple juice, coconut mix, lemon juice, rose liqueur, and Peychaud bitters in a shaker. Add ice and shake. Strain into a festive glass over crushed ice. Top with more crushed ice and snow-cone it (see Speaking of Crushed Ice, page 77). Garnish with dried rose petals, coconut flakes, and fresh lemon zest. Serve with a straw.

ISLAND
LIFE

PARTY
WINE

Island Life

Best enjoyed when . . . *self-care is on the agenda for the day*

Building on the floral notes of Amaro Montenegro, this cocktail is balanced by the earthy calm of amontillado sherry and the dry, clean salinity of fino sherry. I love the oddball combination of sherry and amaro for this, but orange juice is the key. With its tart sweetness, orange juice adds a plump and juicy component if balanced properly.

Serves 1
Glassware: Festive
Ice: Crushed
Garnish: Lavish mint bouquet

1 ounce Amaro Montenegro
¾ ounce amontillado sherry
¾ ounce fino sherry
½ ounce Oat-geat (page 254)
½ ounce dry curaçao
½ ounce fresh orange juice
¼ ounce fresh lime juice

Combine the Amaro Montenegro, amontillado sherry, fino sherry, oat-geat, dry curaçao, orange juice, and lime juice in a shaker. Add 2 ice cubes and give it a short shake. Strain into a festive glass filled with crushed ice. Top with more crushed ice and snow-cone it (see Speaking of Crushed Ice, page 77). Garnish with a lavish mint bouquet. Serve with a straw.

Party Wine

Best enjoyed when . . . *craving reliability*

Oh, this old thing? You know that response you give when you know you look absolutely stunning but don't want to sound like you are your own hype person. That's this drink. It requires a little behind-the-scenes prep, but come showtime, this is shockingly easy to throw together on the spot. Having one person over? Perfect, just quickly whip this up. Having ten people over? Also perfect, as this cocktail is built in the glass, and all you need to do is create a little production line and dole them out.

Serves 1
Glassware: Wineglass
Ice: Cubed
Garnish: None

½ ounce Mulled Wine Reduction (page 256)
2 dashes Angostura bitters
5 ounces dry Lambrusco wine

In a wineglass with cubed ice, build the wine reduction and bitters, followed by the Lambrusco. Stir to incorporate and chill.

Four on the Floor

Best enjoyed when . . . *feeling serious and scholarly, but also there's banana in this cocktail*

I think this cocktail speaks to Suze's incredible versatility. It's an ingredient you rarely see outside the standard-plus-soda or White Negroni. You've heard me sing multiple praises to this bottle of wonder before, but this joyful iteration makes you feel like you just belly-laughed after hearing the dirtiest joke of all time. The rich caramelized banana liqueur, the hints of golden raisins from the sauterne, and the way it's almost dripping overripe tropical fruit from the rum are all in stark contrast to Suze's bright and bitter kick, making this cocktail a wonderfully naughty contradiction.

Serves 1
Glassware: Snifter (chilled!)
Ice: None
Garnish: None

1 ounce Suze apéritif

¾ ounce sauterne

¼ ounce banana liqueur (preferably Tempus Fugit)

½ teaspoon overproof Jamaican rum (preferably Smith & Cross)

Combine the Suze, sauterne, banana liqueur, and rum in a mixing glass. Add ice and stir. Strain into a chilled snifter.

TELL ME MORE

Yes, there is a way to make this drink even yummier! Combine all ingredients with the addition of ¾ ounce of filtered water in a freezer-safe container and chill for 30 minutes (not longer, as the ingredients will start to freeze solid). Then pour it into your chilled snifter and try not to give yourself a brain freeze, because you'll be tempted to gulp.

Rice Dreamz

Best enjoyed when . . . *fantasy meets reality*

Fluffy, whipped clouds of rice pudding covered in a blanket of soft marshmallows. If this is your idea of heaven, well then, congratulations, because you have reached nirvana. Now, in order to achieve nirvana, one does of course have to be willing to put in a little rigorous work behind the scenes. To achieve ultimate cushy-level enlightenment, one must follow proper technique. The process—or if we are going to continue this outrageous metaphor of mine, the path—is strangely satisfying, and that first transformative sip, where your lips just sort of sink into a pillow of downy feathers, is entirely fantastical.

Serves 1

Glassware: Highball

Ice: None

Garnish: Expressed then discarded lemon twist and lime zest

2 ounces unfiltered sake

1 ounce Vanilla Syrup (page 255)

¾ ounce coconut milk

½ ounce fresh lemon juice

½ ounce fresh lime juice

¼ ounce Giffard Lichi-Li Liqueur

4 drops orange flower water

1 organic egg white

Bubbly water, to top

Combine the unfiltered sake, syrup, coconut milk, lemon juice, lime juice, Lichi-Li, orange flower water, and egg white in a shaker. Pre-shake with no ice. Add 5 or 6 cubed ice cubes and shake until the ice is practically dissolved and you can feel the contents of the shaker expanding. The contents of your shaker should be frothy and airy. Strain into a chilled highball glass. Tap the glass on a hard surface to get the cocktail to settle and to remove air bubbles. Add a splash of bubbly water. Tap again on a hard surface. Gradually add more bubbly water, building an egg white head and tapping when necessary. Express a lemon twist over the cocktail then discard. Garnish with freshly grated lime zest. Remember, patience is key in this cocktail. Take your time. There's no rush (even though I know I told you that you are in a race against time just a few chapters ago).

Premier Suite

Best enjoyed when . . . *they upgrade you to first class*

One of my absolutely favorite indulgences is to take a buttery, flaky almond croissant and smear each bite, yes each bite, with a generous glob of additional butter. It's one of those indulgences that I think I've only been able to give in to while staying in a hotel. Therefore, doing so while wearing a plush terry robe post hot bath soak and with the television playing in the background is also mandatory. Anyways, this drink is inspired by that very specific morning at a hotel.

Serves 1

Glassware: Festive

Ice: Crushed

Garnish: Orange and brandied cherry flag
(see page 131)

1½ ounces Lustau Rosé Vermut

1 ounce Pistachio Syrup (page 254)

¾ ounce navy strength gin (preferably
Perry's Tot)

¾ ounce organic heavy cream

Combine the vermouth, syrup, gin, and heavy cream in a shaker. Add ice and shake. Strain into a festive glass over crushed ice. Top with more crushed ice and snow-cone it (see Speaking of Crushed Ice, page 77). Garnish with an orange and brandied cherry flag. Serve with a straw.

Dripping in Rubies

Best enjoyed when . . . *dressed to the nines, out on the town, loving yourself, high-fiving your friends*

This is all about letting yourself be in a festive mood! It's one of those drinks that pretty much anyone with a beating heart will enjoy. You can dance while holding it. You can hug while holding it. It's bubbly, a pretty deep red, and it has drippy cherries by way of Maurin Quina. What's not to like? And best of all, it comes together so easily and is filled to the brim with impactful, warming flavors. Completely suitable for both a snow-covered holiday soirée or summer solstice under a blanket of stars.

Serves 1

Glassware: Wineglass

Ice: Cubed

Garnish: Orange crescent

2 ounces full-bodied red wine

1 ounce Maurin Quina

½ ounce Amaro Averna

¼ ounce Demerara Syrup (page 252)

Dry sparkling white wine, to top

Combine the red wine, Maurin Quina, Averna, and syrup in a wineglass with ice. Top with sparkling wine. Stir to chill and incorporate. Garnish with an orange crescent.

Hot Buttered Sherry

Best enjoyed when . . . *that first cold day of fall finally hits*

No one, not a single person, even those who, like me, loathe cold weather can deny the enchanting combination of a roaring fire and a warming cocktail. There is something wonderful about the simplicity of hot water and booze, but you didn't come here for some spiked hot water; you came here to indulge a bit, so indulge you shall.

Serves 1
Glassware: Mug
Ice: None
Garnish: Grated nutmeg

5 ounces cold-pressed apple cider
1½ ounces Pedro Ximénez sherry
½ ounce vanilla liqueur
1 slice (½ inch thick) Spiced Butter (page 257)

In a saucepan, heat the apple cider. Meanwhile, warm a mug with boiling water. Discard the hot water and add the sherry, vanilla liqueur, and Spiced Butter. Pour the hot apple cider into the mug and stir until the butter is dissolved. Garnish with freshly grated nutmeg.

Candy Rush

Best enjoyed when . . . *wanting to eat your birthday cake straight from the pan with spoons*

Growing up, I loved those hard candies that came in small metal tins. The candies were a variety of fruit flavors, each shaped according to their fruit identity. It's the kind of candy a grandparent would call a *sweety* and are probably always on sale at the drugstore. This drink is an ode to that way-too-sweet sucker from the past, but hopefully it boasts more characteristics than just sugar.

Serves 1
Glassware: Coupe
Ice: None
Garnish: Lemon twist

1½ ounces tawny port
¾ ounce fresh lemon juice
½ ounce Kronan Swedish Punsch
½ ounce Cinnamon Syrup (page 255)
¼ ounce Amaro Ramazzotti
½ teaspoon apricot liqueur

Combine the tawny port, lemon juice, Kronan Swedish Punsch, syrup, Ramazzotti, and apricot liqueur in a shaker. Add ice and shake. Fine-strain into a coupe glass. Garnish with a lemon twist.

Cat Eye

Best enjoyed when . . . *you want big results with minimal effort*

There's a certain elegance and mystery to this cocktail that I can't quite put my finger on (and I will also say that calling my own cocktail elegant and mysterious feels entirely pompous and uncomfortable). But this one is a sort of strange puzzle, and with each sip you discover something new. I love drinks like that. Ones that feel like they are moving with you. That's the brilliance of a complex liqueur such as Strega and the almost animated expression of a well-made fruit brandy working in harmony with some solid, definitive base spirits. I also kind of adore how "easy" this reads on paper but what a complete and utter journey this drink is in real life.

Serves 1

Glassware: Nick and Nora

Ice: None

Garnish: Lemon twist

1½ ounces Lillet Blanc

1 ounce dry vermouth

½ ounce Liquore Strega

½ teaspoon raspberry brandy

Combine the Lillet Blanc, dry vermouth, Strega, and raspberry brandy in a mixing glass. Add ice and stir. Strain into a Nick and Nora glass. Garnish with a lemon twist.

Sunshine Shuttle

Best enjoyed when . . . *you're thinking about that cute diner in an old train car and how they had the best tuna salad platter and sundae*

Honestly, there's not much to say here because all you really need to know is that this cocktail has ice cream. However, since I have your attention, I might as well talk a little about this vermouth-based limoncello and why I'm obsessed with it. If you've ever had the pleasure of sipping on straight-out-of-the-freezer limoncello in a teeny-tiny cordial glass, you'll understand the undeniable joy that comes with this experience. The lemon-bomb liqueur itself is bright yellow, perfectly sweet and viscous, but with a pronounced bitterness. I hope this cocktail-sundae can be shared with people that you simply adore, especially those who appreciate a heavy-handed rainbow sprinkle.

Serves 1

Glassware: Coupe (Or a super fun ice cream sundae glass! Or your fave coffee mug! Or even a V-Martini if you're feeling fancy.)

Ice: None

Garnish: Lemon zest, rainbow sprinkles, brandied cherry

1 overly generous scoop of vanilla ice cream

1½ ounces Vermouth Limoncello (page 260), chilled

1 ounce Salers Gentiane Apéritif, chilled

¼ ounce chamomile grappa liqueur, chilled

Scoop one heaping scoop of vanilla ice cream into your glass of choice. Add the vermouth limoncello, Salers, and chamomile grappa. Garnish with lemon zest, rainbow sprinkles, and a brandied cherry and all of its dripping deliciousness. Serve with a spoon.

Color Me Dazzled

Best enjoyed when . . . *sitting outside during that sweet spot in time when summer blends into fall*

Although popular in France, the Mauresque, a cocktail made by assembling pastis, orgeat, and water over ice, gets little airtime here in the States. It's a strangely delicious concoction and one that I wish I thought of drinking more often. In this little play on that classic, I've replaced the water with freshly pressed Granny Smith apple juice and poured the mix over my fun-loving standby, crushed ice. It's a simple twist that makes a big impact.

Serves 1
Glassware: Festive
Ice: Crushed
Garnish: Apple fan and mint bouquet

3 ounces fresh Granny Smith apple juice
1½ ounces Oat-geat (page 254)
1 ounce pastis

Combine the apple juice, oat-geat, and pastis in a shaker. Add ice and shake. Strain into a festive glass over crushed ice. Top with more crushed ice. Garnish with an apple fan and mint bouquet. Serve with a straw.

TELL ME MORE

At Nitecap, we were always trying to find small little ways to be as environmentally conscious as possible. I had been doing a lot of reading about how almond orchards in California where our almonds for our traditional homemade orgeat came from were wreaking havoc on water supplies and bee colonies. I mentioned my desire to change up our orgeat recipe with a more sustainable and unconventional one, and lo and behold, our then head bartender Arianna Daskauskas came up with oat-geat, which, you guessed it, is made from oat milk. It was sublimely delicious, so delicious that none of our guests missed the almonds. I've changed the recipe a little to make it more suitable for the setting of this book, but let's all thank Ari for this wonderful creation.

Be Right Back

Best enjoyed when . . . *walking in a dreamland*

Scooping a well-made sorbet is so unbelievably satisfying. It's firm with just the right amount of soft give. It curls itself into a perfectly coiled scoop. Your spoon is met with plush resistance, but you're able to make yourself the most glorious bite. When you finally get to taste it, it's an intense sugar rush that is immediately met with a swift wave of tart, tingly fruit. Well, this cocktail is inspired by my fantasy sorbet flavor, and by that I mean it literally doesn't exist, but I wish it did. In the fantasy sorbet isle, this flavor is equally fruity and bitter and tastes like you're walking under a blossoming cherry tree.

Serves 1

Glassware: Double rocks

Ice: Crushed

Garnish: Lavish basil bouquet

1½ ounces red Macvin du Jura

¾ ounce fresh grapefruit juice

¾ ounce fresh lemon juice

½ ounce Aperol

½ ounce Salted Cane Syrup (page 252)

¼ ounce Giffard Rhubarbe Liqueur

2 dashes absinthe

Combine the Macvin du Jura, grapefruit juice, lemon juice, Aperol, syrup, rhubarb liqueur, and absinthe in a shaker. Add ice and shake. Strain into a double rocks glass over crushed ice. Top with more crushed ice and snow-cone it (see Speaking of Crushed Ice, page 77). Garnish with a basil bouquet. Serve with a straw.

Adjacent Move

Best enjoyed when . . . *you initiate a giant group hug*

This devilish cocktail should envelop you like a fleece-lined cashmere blanket. Each sip should relax your shoulders that much more, warming your soul and making that catastrophic run-in with your ex earlier in the day feel like a distant, blurry memory. Also, you were wearing those jeans that make your butt look great, so why are we even calling it catastrophic? Back to the drink, which is served warm and whose spoonful of melted coconut oil goes fantastically well with the notes of golden raisins from the PDC and cinnamon from the aged rum. But don't worry, this drink isn't heavy or overly rich. It's that perfect amount of decadence to help ease the worry of the day. Or the perfect reward after catching another glimpse of your butt in those jeans.

Serves 1

Glassware: Nick and Nora

Ice: None

Garnish: None

1½ ounces Pineau des Charantes

¾ ounce Cardamaro

¾ ounce sweet (red) vermouth

¾ ounce filtered water

½ ounce aged rum

½ teaspoon organic virgin coconut oil

1 pinch kosher salt

Combine the Pineau des Charantes, Cardamaro, sweet vermouth, water, rum, and salt in a small pot. Heat over medium heat until it's just about to start simmering (do not let boil). Stir in the coconut oil. Pour into a Nick and Nora glass. Serve immediately. And it goes without saying, this drink is hot, so hold your glass by the stem.

TELL ME MORE

Cardamaro is a wine-based amaro (store it in the fridge please!) that is made with blessed thistle, also known as Roman thistle, and cardoon, both relatives of the artichoke. It has a slight hint of earthy ginger and the viscosity of a full-bodied sweet vermouth. It's so, so good sipped neat (but chilled), and a small pour makes a big impact in a cocktail.

Easy-Peasy One, Two, Three

LILLET AND CASSIS

Serves 1

Glassware: Double rocks

Ice: Large format

Garnish: Brandied cherries on a spear

2 ounces Lillet Blanc

1 ounce Current Cassis blackcurrant liqueur

In a double rocks glass with large-format ice, add the Lillet Blanc and Current Cassis. Stir to incorporate and chill all ingredients. Garnish with speared brandy cherries.

COFFEE AND SHERRY

Serves 1

Glassware: Mug

Ice: None

Garnish: Freshly grated cinnamon stick

5 ounces hot coffee

¾ ounce Mulled Wine Reduction (page 256)

In a warmed mug, combine the coffee and wine reduction. Stir to incorporate. Garnish with grated cinnamon.

AVERNA AND CREAM

Serves 1

Glassware: Double rocks

Ice: Crushed

Garnish: None

2 ounces Amaro Averna

1 ounce organic heavy cream

In a double rocks glass filled three-quarters of the way with crushed ice, add the Averna followed by the heavy cream. Top with more crushed ice and snow-cone it (see Speaking of Crushed Ice, page 77). Serve with a straw.

COCO MADEIRA AND COMO

Serves 1

Glassware: Highball

Ice: Cubed

Garnish: Orange crescent

2 ounces Toasted Coconut Madeira (page 259)

4 ounces Casamara Club Como soda

In a highball glass with cubed ice, add the coconut-infused madeira and soda. Gently stir to incorporate. Garnish with an orange crescent. Serve with a straw.

AVERNA
AND CREAM

COCO
MADEIRA
AND COMO

LILLET
AND
CASSIS

COFFEE AND
SHERRY

CASAMARA CLUB

COMO

PARTY STARTERS

Gather the people you love, ask them to bring people whom they adore, reacquaint yourself with old friends, and make some new ones. There is nothing quite like communally drinking from a bowl of punch, cheekily served in an oversize sea-shell or the pot you use to boil water—the ritual of sharing is what makes the drink so inviting in the first place. All the recipes here are meant to be crowd-pleasers, kind of like a hot plate of fresh pasta drenched in tomato sauce and generously garnished with Parmesan cheese and fresh hand-torn basil. Who doesn't want that in their life?! This is the chapter that says, "Yes, have a pool party!" "Yes, you absolutely need a disco ball in your bedroom!" and "Yes, absolutely fill your bathtub with ice to keep the case of bubbles cold!" This is the time to break out the fringe, bedazzle that drab pair of jeans, and throw on your party hat. Bowls upon bowls of festive, laugh-together, shimmy-together, BE-together punches coming up. Best of all, many of these punches are designed with ease in mind, so don't be surprised if I'm literally asking you to just combine a few bottles in a bowl.

Invigorating Bowls of Shareable Pleasure, Sure to Set Off a Mesmerizing Fireworks Display

Journey to the Milky Way

Best enjoyed when . . . *needing to be inspired*

Imagine if a flawless glass of white wine ate a hallucinogenic mushroom. As the magical mind trip sets sail, it rides illuminated waves under a glistening moon. "I want to be the most luscious version of myself I can be!" the glass of wine exclaims. The moon smiles with an iridescent, knowing glow. "Fill me with your magic," whispers the glass of wine, mouth agape. A torrential storm of stars starts falling from the sky. Neon rainbows appear and push their way in front of heavy clouds. Happy cows are leaping. Pineapples shine golden in the sun. The glass of wine takes a deep, meditative breath. It is perfect.

Did I go too far? Slash yes, this is a white wine milk punch, and it is really yummy and I'm so excited for you to try it, thanks so much.

Serves 5 or 6

Glassware: Wineglass

Ice: Cubed

Garnish: None

8 ounces organic grass-fed (if possible) whole milk

1 (750 ml) bottle full-bodied white wine, such as a chardonnay

6 ounces sauterne

3 ounces Velvet Falernum liqueur

1½ ounces Pineapple Gum Syrup (page 256)

In a small pot over medium heat, heat the milk until it's just about to simmer. Do not let the milk boil. In a large bowl, combine the white wine, sauterne, Velvet Falernum, and syrup. Add the warmed milk. The milk will immediately begin to curdle as it reacts to the acid in the wine. Let sit for 2 minutes. Strain the mixture through a cheesecloth into another bowl. Discard the solids. Repeat this until all solids are removed, three or four times. Please note that the final result will be cloudy in color (the fat from the milk wash will add texture and dimension). Store in a sealed container and refrigerate until it is cold. When ready to serve, some residue may have settled at the bottom of your container. Gently shake to reincorporate. Serve by pouring 5 ounces over cubed ice in a wineglass or intergalactic chalice as seen here.

Flower Power

Best enjoyed when . . . *partaking in a friendly massage train with your nearest and dearest*

Cucumber juice can quite literally create magic! If the word *freshness* had a taste, it would be just-juiced cucumber. It has the ability to awaken all senses, make you feel completely alert, and transform your mental mindset. Combine that with the bright green herbs in dry vermouth and you've already got yourself a winning duo—that admittedly is a bit predictable. As a little surprise, I've added the almost hay-like flavor of saffron, a true earthy delight. It's just the slightest little crinkle that takes you somewhere unexpected.

Serves 4 to 6

Serving vessel: Pitcher with cubed ice

Glassware: Wineglass

Ice: Cubed

Garnish: 5 cucumber slices (seedless) and 5 lime wheels, plus more for garnishing each glass

8 ounces dry vermouth

4 ounces fresh cucumber juice

3 ounces fresh lime juice

2 ounces Simple Syrup (page 252)

1 ounce Apologue saffron liqueur

16 ounces dry white sparkling wine

In a large shaker, or working in batches with a small shaker, combine the dry vermouth, cucumber juice, lime juice, syrup, and saffron liqueur. Add ice and shake. Strain into a pitcher with cubed ice. Top with sparkling wine. Stir to incorporate all the ingredients. Garnish with cucumber slices and lime wheels.

The Happiest Mulled Wine in All the Land

Best enjoyed when . . . *decorating your house with tinsel and fake snow*

I'm going to say it. If you don't like a mug filled with warming mulled wine, I think you are a person who refuses to let joy into your life. And I say that being a person who throughout this entire book hasn't criticized anyone's personal likes or dislikes, because that is precisely what they are—personal. But when it comes to hot, spiced wine-soup, I have to put my foot down. I'm convinced that the reason you didn't like it is because you had one that was just downright bad, but please give this recipe a whirl, because what is more welcoming than a home that's fragrantly brimming with star anise–laced warmth?

Serves 6 to 8

Serving vessel: Large pot

Glassware: Mug

Ice: None

Garnish: 5 clove-studded orange crescents, plus more for garnishing each glass

1 (750 ml) bottle dry red wine

8 ounces Becherovka

1 ounce orange liqueur

½ cup demerara sugar

10 whole cloves

3 whole star anise

2 cinnamon sticks

1 medium lemon, thinly sliced and deseeded

1 medium orange, thinly sliced and deseeded

In a large pot, combine the red wine, Becherovka, orange liqueur, sugar, cloves, star anise, and cinnamon sticks. Stir over medium heat until the sugar is dissolved. Add the sliced lemon and sliced orange, cover, and let simmer on low heat for at least 30 minutes and up to 1 hour. Remove from the heat and let cool to room temperature, about 15 minutes. Strain out the solids. When ready to serve, reheat over medium heat, making sure never to bring to a boil. Serve in a mug and garnish with a clove-studded orange crescent.

Pool Party

Best enjoyed when . . . *the ground is too hot to walk barefoot on*

This is a truly sessionable cooler. I can't think of anything better to sip on during the day with friends. It's light, refreshing, vegetal, juicy, and most important just super delicious. It also speaks volumes to the beauty of no frills—it's simply fresh ingredients mixed in the right proportions. To make this drink even more perfect, there is no shaking or fine straining or double shaking. Life does not get any easier than this (she says after instructing you to juice three different kinds of fruit).

Serves 4 to 6

Serving vessel: Pitcher with cubed ice

Glassware: Double rocks

Ice: Cubed

Garnish: 7 lime wheels, plus more for garnishing each glass

8 ounces white vermouth (preferably Cinzano bianco)

4 ounces fresh Granny Smith apple juice

3 ounces fresh celery juice

3 ounces fresh lime juice

3 ounces Simple Syrup (page 252)

1 pinch kosher salt

16 ounces bubbly water

In a pitcher filled halfway with cubed ice, combine the white vermouth, apple juice, celery juice, lime juice, syrup, salt, and bubbly water. Top with more ice. Stir to chill and incorporate ingredients. Garnish with lime wheels.

TELL ME MORE

Out of all the white/blanc/bianco vermouths out there, I find that Cinzano makes the driest one. It has beautiful notes of elderflower and clove that pair wonderfully with all the fresh green juice components of this punch.

If These Walls Could Talk

Best enjoyed when . . . *you and your friends are patting each other on the back for a mission accomplished*

In the fantasy world I've created for this punch, Bianca Jagger, Cher, and Diana Ross are just casually throwing things into a hollowed-out disco ball.

"Diana, do you have an apron I can borrow?" asks Cher. "I don't want to get any sugar on this Bob Mackie sweatshirt."

"Darling, I'm just going to throw a couple of these cinnamon sticks into your simple syrup!" exclaims Bianca in another one of her nonchalant moments of brilliance.

"Let me pop these bubbles," says Diana, grabbing an unsuspecting bottle from her icebox. "What a delight. This is a bottle of *red* bubbles!"

"Fabulous," cheers Bianca and Cher in unison.

And, well, there you have it.

Serves 6 to 8

Serving vessel: Punch bowl with mega ice or 4 to 6 large-format ice cubes

Glassware: Wineglass

Ice: Cubed

Garnish: 5 lemon wheels and 5 fresh thyme sprigs, plus more for garnishing each glass

8 ounces amontillado sherry

3 ounces fresh lemon juice

3 ounces Cinnamon Syrup (page 255)

½ ounce peach liqueur

1 (750 ml) bottle dry Lambrusco wine

In a large shaker, or working in batches with a small shaker, combine the amontillado sherry, lemon juice, syrup, and peach liqueur. Add ice and shake. Strain into a punch bowl (or hollowed-out disco ball) with mega ice. Top with Lambrusco and give it a stir. Garnish with lemons wheels and fresh thyme (that Diana had growing by her pool).

Forever More

Best enjoyed when . . . *daydreaming on a snowy afternoon*

In the Hollywood version of what people drink in the French countryside, the story would focus on this apple- and pear-forward, woodsy sparkler. So grab a handful of friends who like to wear silk headscarves and perfectly knit soft cardigans, hop on your vintage bicycles, and pedal on down that cobblestone side street, because there's a pitcher of fruity delights awaiting you in a field of wildflowers.

Serves 8 to 10

Serving vessel: Pitcher with cubed ice

Glassware: Wineglass

Ice: Cubed

Garnish: 7 lemon wheels, plus more for garnishing each glass

4 ounces Bonal Gentiane-Quina

4 ounces pommeau

3 ounces fresh lemon juice

2 ounces unaged pear brandy

2 ounces Vanilla Syrup (page 255)

1 (750 ml) bottle dry white sparkling wine

In a large shaker, or working in batches with a small shaker, combine the Bonal, pommeau, lemon juice, pear brandy, and syrup. Add ice and shake. Strain into a pitcher filled halfway with cubed ice. Add the sparkling wine. Top with ice. Stir to chill and incorporate all ingredients. Garnish with lemon wheels.

Earth Tones

Best enjoyed when . . . *feeling nostalgic for those days when you used to skip rocks at the lake with your fifth grade bestie*

An Aperol Spritz but make it dirty. And I mean that in the best way possible. If you're looking for something a little more rugged, with a bit more grit, this is like the Aperol Spritz ditched the piazza for the mountains and is taking a hike after a rainstorm. Boots are muddied, wild strawberries are foraged, and the sparkling wine is chilled in a . . . um . . . waterfall!

Serves 6 to 8

Serving vessel: Pitcher with cubed ice

Glassware: Double rocks

Ice: Cubed

Garnish: 5 grapefruit crescents, plus more to garnish each glass

10 ounces Beet Aperol (page 258)

2 ounces strawberry liqueur

1 (750 ml) bottle dry white sparkling wine

10 ounces bubbly water

In a pitcher filled halfway with cubed ice, add the beet-infused Aperol and strawberry liqueur. Stir to chill and dilute. Add the sparkling wine and bubbly water and fill the pitcher with more ice. Stir to incorporate all ingredients. Garnish with grapefruit crescents.

Golden Hour

Best enjoyed when . . . *talking about the final chapter in your book club*

This combination hits all the right spots— it's tart, juicy, bubbly, and dry. In fact, this people-pleaser that will certainly unify those from all walks of life is kind of like a teacher's pet, too—it's almost annoyingly easy to drink at any time of day, for any occasion or non-occasion.

Serves 4 to 6

Serving vessel: Punch bowl with mega ice block or 4 to 6 large-format ice cubes

Glassware: Double rocks

Ice: Cubed

Garnish: 5 lemon wheels and 5 grapefruit crescents, plus more for garnishing each glass

6 ounces Pineau des Charantes

2 ounces fresh grapefruit juice

2 ounces amontillado sherry

2 ounces fresh lemon juice

2 ounces Simple Syrup (page 252)

8 ounces dry hard sparkling cider

In a large shaker, or working in batches with a small shaker, combine the Pineau des Charantes, grapefruit juice, sherry, lemon juice, and syrup. Add ice and shake. Strain into a punch bowl with a mega ice block and top with hard sparkling cider. Stir to incorporate ingredients. Garnish with lemon wheels and grapefruit crescents.

Jam Session

Best enjoyed when . . . *you're in a swimsuit with wet hair and sand on your bum*

Introduce acid and bubble into a cocktail with kombucha. This effervescent, living beverage has the sort of bracing acidity you can't quite get enough of, which keeps you engaged and drinking swig after swig. Pair that with the natural sweetness and hydrating power of watermelon juice and you might as well call yourself a self-care expert.

Serves 6 to 8

Serving vessel: Pitcher with cubed ice

Glassware: Double rocks

Ice: Cubed

Garnish: 5 cucumber slices (seedless), plus more for garnishing each glass

1 (750 ml) bottle fino sherry

1 (375 ml) bottle ginger kombucha

12 ounces fresh watermelon juice

In a pitcher filled halfway with ice, add the fino sherry, ginger kombucha, and watermelon juice. Top with more ice. Stir to chill and incorporate ingredients. Garnish with cucumber slices.

Trophy Garden

Best enjoyed when . . . *you need to awaken your soul and restore your faith*

For those days when I am dreaming about a kitchen garden in my future, because who doesn't need a perfect little garden conveniently located right off the side of their kitchen door dedicated to growing the ingredients of a perfect tomato sauce? It all seems very grown-up and lovely and aspirational, and it would be the sort of garden where I would grow fennel and wild elderflower and then just whip something together when unexpected company showed up at my door while my hair is perfectly messy, and I suddenly turn into Nigella Lawson.

Serves 4 to 6

Serving vessel: Pitcher with cubed ice

Glassware: Wineglass

Ice: Cubed

Garnish: 5 thin fennel slices, 8 grapefruit quarters, and 5 lime wheels, plus more for garnishing each glass

6 ounces Salers Gentiane Apéritif

3 ounces fresh grapefruit juice

3 ounces fresh lime juice

3 ounces Fennel Syrup (page 254)

2 ounces St. Germain elderflower liqueur

10 ounces tonic water

In a large shaker, or working in batches with a small shaker, combine the Salers, grapefruit juice, lime juice, syrup, and St. Germain. Add ice and shake. Strain into a pitcher filled halfway with cubed ice. Top with tonic water and add more ice. Stir to chill and incorporate ingredients. Garnish with fennel slices, grapefruit quarters, and lime wheels.

Be Your Own Valentine

Best enjoyed when . . . *freeing yourself from other people's judgment*

There's a certain group of so-called experts in drinking culture who like to shame people for liking delicious things because they've deemed them "basic" (whatever that means). I have a feeling that this seemingly "simple" punch would fall into that category, but don't be bullied into their quite frankly boring, one-dimensional way of thinking. I call on you to embrace this not at all frou-frou, pink as all hell, strawberry-mint dream of a punch, edible flower garnish and all.

Serves 8 to 10

Serving vessel: Pitcher with cubed ice

Glassware: Double rocks

Ice: Cubed

Garnish: 10 strawberry slices, 5 lemon wheels, and 3 edible flowers, plus more for garnishing each glass

3 whole strawberries, leaves removed

10 ounces Lillet Rosé

4 ounces lemon juice

2 ounces Simple Syrup (page 252)

1 ounce Giffard Menthe-Pastille Liqueur

1 (750 ml) bottle dry sparkling rosé wine

In a large shaker, or working in batches with a small shaker, lightly muddle the strawberries. Add the Lillet Rosé, lemon juice, syrup, and menthe-pastille liqueur. Add ice and shake. Fine-strain into your pitcher filled halfway with cubed ice. Top with sparkling rosé. Stir to incorporate ingredients and add more ice. Garnish with strawberry slices, lemon wheels, and edible flowers.

Club Scene

Best enjoyed when . . . that *song comes on*

This is that drink everyone is sipping on at the very end of the party. The music is loud. The makeup is runny. Shoes are off not because people are too wobbly on their feet; they are off so that the dancing can continue. Buttons are undone because shirts can be constricting, and you've still got hours of revelry in you. This cocktail is all about awakening your senses and letting that yuzu juice tingle and tickle your tongue. Also, if I haven't already talked about my love of Suze + passion fruit, let me tell you that it's a combination I love with such intensity that I physically have to restrain myself from putting them into every single cocktail.

Serves 4 to 6

Serving vessel: Punch bowl with mega ice or 4 to 6 large-format ice cubes

Glassware: Wineglass

Ice: Cubed

Garnish: 7 edible flowers, plus more for garnishing each glass

8 ounces dry white wine

4 ounces Suze apéritif

2 ounces Giffard Fruit de la Passion Liqueur

2 ounces fresh Meyer lemon juice

2 ounces Honey Syrup (page 253)

10 ounces bubbly water

In a large shaker, or working in batches with a small shaker, combine the white wine, Suze, passion fruit liqueur, Meyer lemon juice, and syrup. Add ice and shake. Strain into a punch bowl with mega/large-format ice. Add the bubbly water. Stir to incorporate all ingredients. Garnish with edible flowers.

TELL ME MORE

I opted for Meyer lemons in this cocktail, as they tend to be more succulent and not quite as acidic as regular lemons. There's also something almost piney about them, which is lovely when combined with the Suze.

Smash Up

Best enjoyed when . . . *listening to the George Michael Christmas album (an activity not limited to the holiday season)*

Blood oranges are technically in season for like twenty-four hours a year, and I look forward to it every time. There is, strangely, something quite vampire-esque about the taste, a sort of metallic, very mineral-forward, sweet juiciness. When combined with either lemon or lime juice, it takes on all sorts of bright, cheerful characteristics as well, while still maintaining some of its mystery. It's this flavor combination that drew me to pair it with East India sherry, a sherry that feels luxurious as it's so full of seductive deep raisin notes.

Serves 6 to 8

Serving vessel: Punch bowl with mega ice or 4 to 6 large-format ice cubes

Glassware: Double rocks

Ice: Cubed

Garnish: 5 lime wheels, 5 blood orange crescents, and freshly grated cinnamon, plus more for garnishing each glass

8 ounces East India sherry

4 ounces white rum (preferably Owney's)

4 ounces fresh pineapple juice

3 ounces fresh lime juice

3 ounces fresh blood orange juice

2 ounces Simple Syrup (page 252)

16 ounces dry Lambrusco wine

In a large shaker, or working in batches with a small shaker, combine the East India sherry, rum, pineapple juice, lime juice, blood orange juice, and syrup. Add ice and shake. Strain into a punch bowl with mega/large-format ice. Top with Lambrusco. Stir to incorporate all ingredients. Garnish with lime wheels, blood orange crescents, and freshly grated cinnamon.

TELL ME MORE

Owney's is a woman-owned company that produces rum in Brooklyn that is all about ripe, earthy, tropical fruit. Think guava, mango, caramelized banana. I loved how these notes interact with the rest of the ingredients here.

No Bad Days

Best enjoyed when . . . *sitting in your favorite person's lap*

The idea behind this one is that it's almost too easy to make, so it's perfectly acceptable for one of the ingredients to be an infusion. Each ingredient on its own, while supremely delicious, is what I like to describe as soft. But when brought together, they are transformed into a vibrant tour de force. I simply adore this cocktail and created it with a wide range of palates in mind. It's kind of like a peace offering between the Martini drinker and the Sour drinker, brought together by the harmony of a big bowl of booze.

Serves 10 to 14

Serving vessel: Extra-large punch bowl with mega ice or 6 to 8 large-format ice cubes

Glassware: Double rocks

Ice: Cubed

Garnish: 15 lemon wheels

1 (750 ml) bottle dry sparkling wine, chilled

1 (750 ml) bottle Thai Basil Blanc Vermouth (page 258), chilled

1 (750 ml) bottle manzanilla sherry, chilled

750 ml fresh watermelon juice

In an extra-large punch bowl over a mega ice block, combine the sparkling wine, basil-infused vermouth, manzanilla sherry, and watermelon juice. Stir to incorporate all ingredients. Garnish with lemon wheels.

Get It Done

Best enjoyed when .... *licking drippy juices of whatever delicious sandwich is your favorite from the side of your hand*

I remember being introduced to the art of the Michelada pretty late into my bartending journey, when I started working behind the bar at Mayahuel. While Mayahuel certainly didn't invent the Michelada (a traditional Mexican beverage dating back almost one hundred years), the bartenders there were well versed in coming up with some pretty epic variations. In this version, I've replaced the tomato element with a smoky ancho chile by way of Ancho Reyes, which adds a beautiful earthy layer to this otherwise refreshing, sharp cocktail. It's the perfect partner to an extravagant snack setup.

Serves 6 to 8

Serving vessel: Pitcher with cubed ice

Glassware: Double rocks with optional salt rim

Ice: Cubed

Garnish: 7 lime wheels, plus more to garnish each glass

2 (12-ounce) bottles Mexican lager beer, such as Modelo Especial

4 ounces fresh pineapple juice

3 ounces Ancho Reyes Ancho Chile Liqueur

2 ounces fresh lime juice

2 ounces agave nectar

In a pitcher filled halfway with cubed ice, add the beer. Let settle. In a large shaker, or working in batches with a small shaker, combine the pineapple juice, Ancho Reyes, lime juice, and agave nectar. Add ice and shake. Strain into the pitcher with the beer. Fill with more ice and stir to incorporate ingredients. Garnish with lime wheels.

Kiss 'n' Tell

Best enjoyed when . . . *it's a classy sort of soirée*

Maybe you've been trying to find an excuse to wear your feather-adorned kitten heels. Or maybe it's your velvet slippers. Whichever footwear choice speaks to you most is the kind of mood you need to bring to serving this Martini-esque crowd sipper. If you happen to have a sunken living room, you get bonus points.

Serves 4 to 6

Serving vessel: Pitcher with cubed ice

Glassware: Mini V-Martini or mini Nick and Nora

Garnish: Cocktail onion, in glass only

10 ounces dry vermouth

6 ounces Salers Gentiane Apéritif

3 ounces Good Vodka (like the actual brand Good Vodka, not just good vodka)

5 dashes Scrappy's Celery Bitters

In a pitcher, combine the dry vermouth, Salers, vodka, and bitters. Add ice and stir to chill and dilute. Imagine you are quite literally making a large-format stirred cocktail. Serve by straining 3 ounces into a glass with a cocktail onion.

Easy-Peasy One, Two, Three

WINE AND PEAR

Serves 4 to 6

Serving vessel:
  Wine decanter

Glassware:
  Wineglass

Ice: Cubed

Garnish: None

1 (750 ml) bottle Auslese Riesling (chilled to the bone!)

1 mini (50 ml) bottle Clear Creek Pear Brandy* (chilled to the bone!)

Pour the bottle of wine into the decanter. Invert the mini bottle of pear brandy into the decanter. Pour into ice-filled wineglasses. Delight in life and everything it has to offer.

* If you can't source the mini bottle of pear brandy, you can of course jigger out the amount and pour it into the decanter with the wine.

AMARO AND BUBBLES

Serves 4 to 6

Serving vessel:
  Pitcher with cubed ice

Glassware:
  Wineglass

Ice: Cubed

Garnish: 5 lemon wheels, plus more for each glass

1 (750 ml) bottle dry Lambrusco wine

5 ounces Amaro Ramazzotti

In a pitcher filled with ice, add the Lambrusco and Ramazzotti. Stir to chill and incorporate. Add more ice if needed. Garnish with lemon wheels.

CELLO AND PARTAYYY

Serves 4 to 6

Serving vessel:
  Pitcher with cubed ice

Glassware:
  Wineglass

Ice: Cubed

Garnish: Olive

1 (750 ml) bottle dry sparkling wine

10 ounces Vermouth Limoncello (page 260)

In a pitcher filled with ice, add the sparkling wine and vermouth. Stir to chill and incorporate. Garnish each glass with an olive on a pick.

AMARO AND
BUBBLES

WINE
AND
PEAR

CELLO AND
PARTAYYY

Whether your body is asking you to take a break from those spritzes, or if alcohol with any amount of ABV just isn't your thing, there's no good reason that cocktails without alcohol shouldn't be given the same thought and integrity as those with it. One thing I always find mildly offensive is that zero proof either means salad bar cocktails or lemonade—wait for it—topped with ginger ale, what an innovation! While I wouldn't shun simplicity, because I very much respect and admire simplicity, we deserve more than the same ginger-spiked lemonade over and over again. This chapter, like all others in the book, is built on the same foundation of classic cocktails, but in place of a fortified wine (which technically stand in for full-proof booze), I've called upon our juicy modifiers to take the lead. These are cocktails with an equal amount of complexity and conviviality. They are the life of the party and shun convention. So I call upon you to embrace all the flavors and styles the world has to offer, while making sure you store up enough energy to continue the good fight.

For a Good Time, Anytime, Delightful, Dance-Inducing Sips sans Alcohol, Intended to Tickle Your Tail Feathers

Mental Note

Best enjoyed when . . . *trying to find the end of a rainbow*

The awe-inspiring color of this drink is vibrant enough to wake you from the depths of a deep, satisfying slumber. The first sip is intended to give you a little spark of electricity that you can feel all the way down in your toes. Tart but unwaveringly earthy, it's equally comforting and life-giving. And then of course there is our bestie, crushed ice, which makes this combination taste that much better. Go ahead and choose joy today.

Serves 1

Glassware: Festive

Ice: Crushed

Garnish: Grapefruit crescent and lemon wheel

2 ounces fresh grapefruit juice

1 ounce fresh lemon juice

¾ ounce fresh beet juice

½ ounce Vanilla Syrup (page 255)

1 heaping bar spoon of raspberry preserves (the kind with seeds!)

Combine the grapefruit juice, lemon juice, beet juice, syrup, and raspberry preserves in a shaker. Add ice and shake. Fine-strain into a festive glass over crushed ice. Top with more crushed ice and snow-cone it (see Speaking of Crushed Ice, page 77). Garnish with a grapefruit crescent and lemon wheel. Serve with a straw.

T.B.D.

Best enjoyed when . . . *boredom forces you out of the house and into an adventure*

When you plan a surprise party for someone, there are only two ways it can go. Either they will love it, be overcome with happy warm feelings, and passionately kiss you as they fight back tears, or they will give you a look so sharp it cuts your soul, and you feel instant regret for having devoted days of your life to bring this moment to fruition. Well, just ignore the possibility of the second outcome, and sink deep into scenario number one. That's this drink. It's your favorite person's birthday and it's going to be totally great. This drink starts out totally lovely, perhaps even comfortingly predictable, and then you get a hit of the yuzu koshu and your day has suddenly turned into a past-midnight fête.

Serves 1

Glassware: Highball

Ice: None

Garnish: Expressed then discarded orange twist

2 ounces fresh orange juice

1½ ounces Vanilla Syrup (page 255)

¾ ounce fresh lime juice

¾ ounce organic heavy cream

1 teaspoon green yuzu kosho

1 organic egg white

Bubbly water, to top

Combine the orange juice, syrup, lime juice, heavy cream, yuzu kosho, and egg white in a shaker. Pre-shake with no ice. Add ice and shake for at least 1 minute. Strain into a highball glass and top with bubbly water. Express an orange twist over the cocktail then discard.

TELL ME MORE

Yuzu kosho is a Japanese condiment made from chiles that are fermented with salt and the juice and zest of yuzu. Available in both green and red varieties, the green is made from green chiles and the red, yup, you guessed it, from red chiles. It packs a serious punch and is equal parts spicy, salty, and tart.

Morning Routine

Best enjoyed when . . . *eating a stack of pancakes covered in powdered sugar*

The world's most delightful glass of grown-up milk. And even though you are an adult, I do feel the need to warn you that the garnish is indeed on fire, so please avoid planting your face on it.

Serves 1
Glassware: Double rocks
Ice: Crushed
Garnish: Flaming cinnamon stick

4 ounces barista-quality oat milk (preferably Oatly)
½ ounce Cinnamon Syrup (page 255)
½ teaspoon matcha powder
2 drops rose flower water

Combine the oat milk, syrup, and matcha powder in shaker. Add 2 ice cubes and shake. Strain into a double rocks glass over crushed ice. Top with more crushed ice and snow-cone it (see Speaking of Crushed Ice, page 77). Tuck a cinnamon stick into the crushed ice and light it on fire. Blow out the flame and let the cinnamon stick smoke. Serve with a straw. And please, don't put the straw right next to the smoking HOT cinnamon stick.

See You on Wednesday

Best enjoyed when . . . *happily finding yourself on a weekend getaway in Palm Springs*

Do you ever take that first big satisfying sip of a Margarita and think to yourself, "This tastes life-giving and cleansing!" If you answered with a resounding YES, then this is the cure to your craving. This is every juicy, spicy, savory dream wrapped up in a festive salt-speckled bow. I often find drinking celery juice on its own a little, shall we say, lacking, so the gooey yum of the agave nectar is there to give this drink some texture and weight.

Serves 1

Glassware: Double rocks

Ice: Large format

Garnish: Tajín salt rim and celery spear

2 jalapeño slices

1 cilantro sprig

¾ ounce agave nectar

3 ounces fresh celery juice

1 ounce fresh lime juice

3 drops Salt Solution (page 261)

At the bottom of a shaker, muddle the jalapeño, cilantro, and agave nectar. Add the celery juice, lime juice, and salt solution. Add ice and shake. Fine-strain into a Tajín-rimmed double rocks glass over large-format ice. Garnish with a celery spear.

Dreaming in Pink

Best enjoyed when . . . *having just crossed a desert*

Watermelon juice is basically the universe's gift to humans who are parched but bored by water. When watermelon is ultra-ripe, all you have to do is look at it and it basically juices itself. I love a touch of savory with pretty much anything sweet, and a little touch of a neutral yet flavorful vinegar can make such a dramatic impact. Throw a few fresh, equally-in-season basil leaves into the mix and you can basically just sit back and let Mother Nature do her thing. And if you're not already wearing a straw hat, I highly recommend putting one on.

Serves 1

Glassware: Highball

Ice: Cubed

Garnish: Smoked-salt rim, lime wheel, and basil bouquet

5 ounces fresh watermelon juice

1 tablespoon unseasoned rice vinegar

5 or 6 basil leaves

Gently muddle the basil leaves at the bottom of your glass. In a shaker, combine the watermelon juice, rice vinegar, and basil leaves. Add ice and shake. Strain into a smoked salt–rimmed highball glass over cubed ice. Garnish with a lime wheel and fresh basil bouquet. Serve with a straw.

GO-GO TIME

HAPPY PLACE,
PAGE 247

SHOCK VALUE,
PAGE 240

Go-Go Time

Best enjoyed when . . . *you need a little zing to get you going*

When I was a teenager, spiced chai became all the rage among my group of friends. We would buy that almost unbearably sweet chai concentrate in a paper carton, mix it with milk, talk about our feelings, and absolutely not ever smoke a cigarette with it. This drink calls for chilled, brewed chai, and it's a choose-your-own-adventure-type call. If you want to keep it light, simply brew your tea in hot water, or, for something more decadent, make a milk tea by steeping your tea in the warmed milk of your choice, though I recommend full-fat cow's milk or macadamia milk, which pairs lovely with the pineapple.

Serves 1
Glassware: Festive
Ice: Crushed
Garnish: Coconut flakes and fresh lime zest

3 ounces chilled brewed spiced chai
1 ounce coconut milk
¾ ounce Pineapple Gum Syrup (page 256)
1 fresh lime leaf

Combine the chai, coconut milk, syrup, and lime leaf in a shaker. Add ice and shake. Fine-strain into a festive footed tulip glass over crushed ice. Garnish with coconut flakes and lime zest. Serve with a straw.

TELL ME MORE

Lime leaves, also known as Makrut lime leaves, are the leaves of, you guessed it, the Makrut lime tree, native to Southeast Asia. The leaves are distinctively aromatic and are often used in curries and stews. Think of it as a sort of bay leaf in terms of usage. Uncooked, I love using them in cocktails, where simply shaking one single leaf into a drink will completely transform its flavor profile and add a beautiful brightness.

Shock Value

Best enjoyed when . . . *investing in your future*

Once I passed the thirty-years-old mark, I, like many adults before me, invested in my first pair of well-made jeans. Oh, the difference! I wasn't tugging them back up every two seconds, their material felt sturdy, my bum never looked better. And that brings me to lemonade. Who doesn't love lemonade? But just as with jeans, there's lemonade and there's LEMONADE. I love mine with a higher-than-usual lemon-to-sugar ratio, because I want my face to scrunch up as if I were taking a generous bite from a lemon wedge. This recipe is the upgrade you've been looking for, even if you are under thirty.

Serves 1
Glassware: Double rocks
Ice: Cubed
Garnish: Lemon wheel

1 whole green cardamom pod
2 ounces fresh lemon juice
½ ounce Honey Syrup (page 253)
San Bitter or other nonalcoholic red bitter soda, to top

At the bottom of a shaker, lightly muddle the cardamom pod until it has broken apart. Add the lemon juice and syrup. Add ice and shake. Fine-strain into a double rocks glass filled with cubed ice and top with the red bitter soda. Garnish with a lemon wheel.

Sweet Relief

Best enjoyed when . . . *wanting to feel your fingertips and toes tingle*

My cure for the Something & Tonic craving that packs a flavorful punch. It's ideal for sipping while feeling at peace, dancing under a flickering strobe light. But also equally as enjoyable sunbathing, bum out, on your rooftop. An invigorating experience you'll feel in your whole body.

Serves 1
Glassware: Highball
Ice: Cubed
Garnish: Lime wheel and lemon wheel

2 ounces Salted Lemon-Lime Cordial (page 253)
½ ounce Cinnamon Syrup (page 255)
1 fresh curry leaf
Tonic water, to top

Combine the lemon-lime cordial, syrup, and curry leaf in a shaker. Add ice and shake. Fine-strain into a highball glass with cubed ice. Top with tonic water. Garnish with lime wheel and lemon wheel. Serve with a straw.

Shimmy Right

Best enjoyed when ... *the music is good, the juice is flowing, the people are smiling*

This drink is inspired by my love of grilled red bell peppers. Large get-togethers at our house in the summer almost always mean a large platter of grilled vegetables. My favorite is always the pepper, smothered in good olive oil and plenty of salt. I had experimented with grilling the peppers for this drink before juicing, but of course that meant sacrificing their brilliant sweetness and crispness, which would have been a real bummer to lose. Enter hickory liquid smoke. I was able to keep everything tasting fresh while adding a powerful baseline of gritty smokiness.

Serves 1
Glassware: Double rocks
Ice: Large format
Garnish: Lemon wheel

2 ounces fresh red bell pepper juice

1 ounce fresh lemon juice

¾ ounce Pomegranate Grenadine (page 252)

½ ounce Simple Syrup (page 252)

10 drops hickory liquid smoke

Combine the bell pepper juice, lemon juice, pomegranate grenadine, syrup, and liquid smoke in a shaker. Add ice and shake. Strain into a double rocks glass over large-format ice. Garnish with a lemon wheel.

Vitamin Parade

Best enjoyed when . . . *in full recovery mode*

Pure liquid fortification. Combining two of my favorites here, freshly pressed carrot and pineapple juices, with the clean spicy notes of the ginger makes this an ideal companion to raucous conversation or a lively, straight-out-of-bed solo morning. Your body should feel good about drinking this, look forward to it, maybe even crave it so much that you make it part of your weekly rotation of self-care rituals.

Serves 1

Glassware: Fizz

Ice: None

Garnish: Expressed then discarded lemon twist and pineapple wedge

2 ounces fresh carrot juice

¾ ounce fresh pineapple juice

¾ ounce fresh lemon juice

½ ounce Cinnamon Syrup (page 255)

1 organic egg white

Ginger beer, to top

Combine the carrot juice, pineapple juice, lemon juice, syrup, and egg white in a shaker. Pre-shake with no ice. Add ice and shake. Fine-strain into a fizz glass. Top with ginger beer. Express a lemon twist over cocktail then discard. Garnish with a pineapple wedge.

Adult Supervision

Best enjoyed when . . . *sitting under the shade of a giant umbrella*

I think I could sip on this all day, every day. There's something strikingly elegant about this drink. But at the same time, it certainly doesn't take itself too seriously. Inspired by my love of Shirley Temples as a child, which I only got to drink once a year when we visited my grandmother and had dinner at the Golden Dragon, where we feasted on paper-wrapped chicken and thick sauce-drenched rice noodles.

Serves 1
Glassware: Wineglass
Ice: Cubed
Garnish: 3 lemon wheels

1 ounce Raspberry Syrup (page 255)
¾ ounce white verjus
Bubbly water, to top

In a wineglass filled with cubed ice, build the syrup, verjus, and bubbly water. Stir to chill and incorporate all ingredients. Garnish with 3 lemon wheels.

Hit List

Best enjoyed when . . . *finding the smell of sunscreen alluring*

There's not much I need to say about this drink except that it's as refreshing as walking into the walk-in cooler during a hot summer shift. Juicy and tart with a little kick from the fresh ginger, it's easy to lose track of how many you've drunk, thus I've made this sans alcohol.

Serves 1
Glassware: Festive
Ice: Cubed
Garnish: Lime wedge

2 ounces fresh pineapple juice
½ ounce fresh lime juice
¼ ounce Ginger Syrup (page 254)
Nonalcoholic lager, to top

Combine the pineapple juice, lime juice, and syrup in a shaker. Add 2 ice cubes and shake. Strain into a festive glass with cubed ice. Top with nonalcoholic lager. Garnish with a lime wedge.

Happy Place

Best enjoyed when . . . *finishing a big meal with friends but you're still hungry*

You know what I love? Salad dressing. I'm not talking creamy ranch or Caesar (though my obsession with finding the perfect Caesar salad is pretty infamous among my circle of friends). I'm talking vinaigrette. I like my dressing to be so vinegary that it gives me a shiver. I often combine different vinegars on one salad, then different mustards and honeys, too. The best bite of salad is when the salad is gone, and you get to grab a spoon and just drink the veggie-soaked puddle of dressing remaining in the bottom of the bowl. This drink is my socially acceptable salad-dressing juice cocktail.

Serves 1
Glassware: Highball
Glass: Cubed
Garnish: Pickled carrot and lime wedge

3 ounces fresh carrot juice
¾ ounce fresh lime juice
½ ounce Salted Cane Syrup (page 252)
½ ounce pickle brine
1 tablespoon prepared horseradish

Combine the carrot juice, lime juice, syrup, pickle brine, and horseradish in a shaker. Add ice and shake. Strain* into a highball glass over fresh ice. Garnish with a pickled carrot and a lime wedge. Serve with a straw.

*Pssst. So, you know how I told you to make sure the gate on your hawthorn strainer is always tightly closed. Well, here's the exception to that rule. In fact, make sure that the gate is *not* closed to ensure that all of the horseradish makes it into the glass.

Easy-Peasy One, Two, Three

CARROT AND BITTER

Serves 1

Glassware: Highball

Ice: Cubed

Garnish: Lime wedge

2 ounces carrot juice

3 ounces San Bitter or other nonalcoholic red bitter soda

In a highball glass with cubed ice, add the carrot juice and soda. Gently stir to incorporate. Garnish with a lime wedge. Serve with a straw.

MANGO AND TONIC

Serves 1

Glassware: Wineglass

Ice: Cubed

Garnish: Lime wheel

1 ounce mango vinegar

5 ounces Fever Tree Mediterranean Tonic Water

In a wineglass with cubed ice, add the mango vinegar and tonic water. Gently stir to incorporate. Garnish with a lime wheel.

BEET AND GINGER

Serves 1

Glassware: Highball

Ice: Crushed

Garnish: Lime wedge

½ ounce beet juice

5 ounces ginger beer

In a highball glass with crushed ice, add the ginger beer followed by the beet juice. Garnish with a lime wedge. Serve with a straw.

TELL ME MORE

Mango vinegar sounds pretty niche, but is actually amazingly versatile. Some are made by steeping ripe mangoes in a vinegar base while others are made by literally adding mango juice to vinegar, and all that I've come across are as delicious on a salad, used in a marinade, or even drizzled on a dessert.

BEET AND
GINGER

MANGO
AND TONIC

CARROT
AND BITTER

SYRUPS AND
INFUSIONS

Not all syrup and infusion recipes are created equal. These versions are the truest expression of whatever flavor I'm trying to capture. A well-made syrup has the ability to let the other flavors sing, fold components together, and highlight nuanced and subtle notes. They can enhance texture or just be a trusty support system for other ingredients. A great infusion can help you see a familiar bottle in a whole new light. It can act as a flavor enhancer or shine as the headliner. Some of these recipes take time; others come together in a flash. Either way, the fruits of your labor will be rewarded, as there is nothing quite like using fresh, high-quality ingredients to up your cocktail-making game.

I always like to encourage people to make the recipes using ingredients that are at their seasonal peak. Of course, this is just a suggestion, not a rule, and like anyone, I understand the powerful urge to escape the icy chills of winter with a transportive cocktail.

In an effort to truly capture some of those notes, you'll see that I use a sous-vide method, or immersion circulator, to extract flavor for many of my recipes. It's a method I was introduced to by my partner Alex Day at Nitecap (yeah, he has lots of good ideas!). By using a controlled environment, you can create the ideal climate to extract all the raw, bright flavors of your ingredients. I use reusable, heat-resistant, food-safe silicone bags, as they are a great alternative to onetime-use sealable bags. Although I personally think that certain syrups or infusions are best when made using an immersion circulator, I do recognize that this is a specialty piece of equipment that not everyone has, which is why I will always offer an alternative, more conventional method. One final note: If a syrup recipe calls for any kind of fresh juice as an ingredient, please make sure to fine-strain it before adding.

Combine the demerara sugar and water in a blender and blend until the sugar has completely dissolved, 2 to 3 minutes. Store in a sealed container in the fridge for up to 1 month.

SALTED CANE SYRUP

Makes about 2 cups

300 grams organic cane sugar

150 grams filtered water

3 grams kosher salt

Combine the cane sugar, water, and salt in a blender and blend until the sugar and salt are completely dissolved, 2 to 3 minutes. Store in a sealed container in the fridge for up to 1 month.

POMEGRANATE GRENADINE

Makes about 2 cups

Note: This is not your bottled red sugar goop! In fact, this grenadine is bright and tart and, yes, fantastic in a Shirley Temple.

400 grams 100 percent pomegranate juice, such as POM

400 grams white sugar

2 grams citric acid

5 drops orange extract

Combine all the ingredients in a blender and blend until the sugar and citric acid have dissolved, 2 to 3 minutes. Store in a sealed container in the fridge for up to 2 weeks.

Syrups

SIMPLE SYRUP

Makes about 2 cups

200 grams white sugar

200 grams filtered water

Combine the sugar and water in a blender and blend until the sugar is completely dissolved, 2 to 3 minutes. Store in a sealed container in the fridge for up to 1 month.

DEMERARA SYRUP

Makes about 2 cups

300 grams (packed) demerara sugar

150 grams filtered water

HONEY SYRUP

Makes about 1½ cups

1 cup honey

½ cup filtered water

In a medium bowl, combine the honey and water. Using a whisk, combine until the honey has dissolved in the water. Store in a sealed container in the fridge for up to 4 weeks.

Note: Different honeys have different flavors. You'll notice that I didn't call for a specific honey type in this recipe. That's because I leave it to you to explore the wide world of honey! Personally, I love acacia honey in my cocktails, as it's delicate and gently floral with an almost butter-like softness to it. Linden honey has much more structure to it without overpowering the other ingredients. And have we talked about cherry blossom honey?! OH MY.

SALTED LEMON-LIME CORDIAL

Makes about 3 cups

300 grams lemon juice

300 grams lime juice

200 grams white sugar

3 grams kosher salt

Peeled zest of 5 lemons

Peeled zest of 5 limes

Combine the lemon juice, lime juice, sugar, and salt in a medium bowl and whisk until the sugar and salt are dissolved. Add the lemon and lime zests to an airtight container. Add the juice and sugar mixture to the zests. Cover and let sit in the fridge for 24 hours. Strain through a chinois. Store in a sealed container for up to 2 weeks.

Note: The idea behind this cordial came out of a desire not to waste juices left over at the end of a shift at Nitecap, as we juiced fresh daily. I came up with this recipe to give that juice another life, and we always found a way to incorporate it into our menus.

MANGO-HONEY SYRUP

Makes about 1 cup

¾ cup mango puree

¼ cup Honey Syrup (left)

Combine the puree and honey syrup in a small bowl and mix. Store in a sealed container in the fridge for up to 2 weeks.

COCONUT MIX

Makes about 1 cup

¾ cup cream of coconut, such as Coco Lopez

¼ cup coconut milk

In a medium bowl, combine the cream of coconut and coconut milk. Using a whisk, mix until smooth.* Store in a sealed container in the fridge for up to 4 weeks.

* Is your coconut milk stubborn and chunky? Then mix this in a blender instead.

GINGER SYRUP

Makes about 2 cups

150 grams fresh ginger juice (from about ¾ pound fresh ginger)

300 grams white sugar

Combine the ginger juice and sugar in a blender and blend until the sugar has dissolved, 4 to 5 minutes. Store in a sealed container in the fridge for up to 2 weeks.*

* The ginger syrup won't go bad in 2 weeks, but those incredible fresh, earthy, and spicy notes from the juiced ginger will start mellowing out, so I recommend using it up as fast as you can.

FENNEL SYRUP

Makes about 2 cups

200 grams fresh fennel juice (from about 2 fennel bulbs)

100 grams white sugar

Combine the fennel juice and sugar in a blender and blend until the sugar has dissolved, 2 to 3 minutes. Store in a sealed container in the fridge for up to 3 days.

GREEN BELL PEPPER SYRUP

Makes about 2 cups

200 grams fresh green bell pepper juice (from 2 to 3 whole bell peppers)

200 grams white sugar

Combine the pepper juice and sugar in a blender and blend until the sugar has dissolved, 2 to 3 minutes. Store in a sealed container in the fridge for up to 3 days.

OAT-GEAT

Makes about 2 cups

200 grams Oatly or other barista-quality oat milk

200 grams white sugar

1 ounce amaretto liqueur

1 ounce Amaro Nonino

Combine the oat milk and sugar in a blender and blend until the sugar has dissolved, 2 to 3 minutes. Add the amaretto and Amaro Nonino and blend for an additional 30 seconds. Store in a sealed container in the fridge for up to 2 weeks.

PISTACHIO SYRUP

Makes about 4 cups

200 grams shelled pistachio nuts

300 grams filtered water, plus additional for making the pistachio milk

400 grams white sugar

1 ounce vanilla liqueur

½ ounce rose liqueur

First, make a pistachio milk. In a sealed container, cover the pistachio nuts with filtered water, making sure they are fully submerged. Let soak for at least 8 hours and up to 24 hours. Strain the water and remove the skins of the pistachio nuts. In a blender, blitz the nuts until they form a paste. Add 300 grams filtered water and blend until combined. Strain the mixture through a nut bag. You should be able to extract 400 grams of pistachio milk from the mixture. In a blender, combine the nut milk and sugar and blend until the sugar is dissolved, 3 to 4 minutes. Add the vanilla liqueur and rose liqueur. Blend for an additional 30 seconds. Store in a sealed container for up to 2 weeks.

VANILLA SYRUP

Makes about 2 cups

500 grams Simple Syrup (page 252)
4 grams Tahitian vanilla extract
2 grams lactic acid (see page 75)
1 pinch kosher salt

In a medium bowl, combine the syrup, vanilla extract, lactic acid, and salt. Using a whisk, combine until the lactic acid and salt are dissolved. Store in a sealed container in the fridge for up to 4 weeks.

ORANGE CREAM SYRUP

Makes about 3 cups

200 grams Vanilla Syrup (recipe above)
100 grams orange juice

Combine the syrup and orange juice in a medium bowl and mix. Store in a sealed container in the fridge for up to 1 week. The syrup won't necessarily go "bad" after a week, but the orange flavor will certainly lose its luster.

RASPBERRY SYRUP

Makes about 2 cups

500 grams Simple Syrup (page 252)
150 grams raspberries
2 grams citric acid

Fill a basin with water and set an immersion circulator to 135°F. Meanwhile, combine the syrup, raspberries, and citric acid in a sealable, heatproof silicone bag, making sure to push out all the air. Once the circulator has reached the desired temperature, place the sealed bag in the water bath. Let cook for 2 hours. Once done, transfer the infusion to an ice bath until it reaches room temperature. Strain through a nut bag. Store in a sealed container in the fridge for up to 2 weeks.

No sous vide?
In a medium, heat-safe bowl, gently muddle the raspberries. Add the syrup and citric acid. Cover the top of the bowl tightly with plastic wrap. Place the covered bowl over a large pot filled with 3 to 5 inches of water, making sure the bowl doesn't touch the water (you are essentially creating a double boiler). Cook over medium heat for 1 hour. Remove from heat and let cool. Strain through a nut bag.

CINNAMON SYRUP

Makes about 2 cups

500 grams Simple Syrup (page 252)
10 grams Saigon cinnamon bark

Fill a basin with water and set an immersion circulator to 135°F. Meanwhile, combine the syrup and cinnamon bark in a sealable, heatproof silicone bag, making sure to push out all the air. Once the circulator has reached the desired temperature, place the sealed bag in the water bath. Let cook for 2 hours. Once done, transfer the infusion to an ice bath until it reaches room temperature. Strain through a chinois.

Store in a sealed container in the fridge for up to 2 weeks.

No sous vide?

In a medium, heat-safe bowl, combine the syrup and cinnamon bark. Cover the top of the bowl tightly with plastic wrap. Place the covered bowl over a large pot filled with 3 to 5 inches of water, making sure the bowl doesn't touch the water (you are essentially creating a double boiler). Cook over medium heat for 1 hour. Remove from heat and let cool. Strain through a chinois.

PINEAPPLE GUM SYRUP

Makes about 2 cups

250 grams white sugar

15 grams gum arabic

2 grams citric acid

250 grams canned pineapple juice*

Fill a basin with water and set an immersion circulator to 140°F. In a blender, combine the sugar, gum arabic, and citric acid and mix on low until all the ingredients are incorporated. Begin to add the pineapple juice and blend until all the dry ingredients have dissolved. Add the mixture to a sealable, heatproof silicone bag, making sure to push out all the air. Once the circulator has reached the desired temperature, place the sealed bag in the water bath. Let cook for 2 hours. Once done, transfer the infusion to an ice bath until it reaches room temperature. Store in a sealed container in the fridge for up to 2 weeks.

No sous vide?

In a medium, heat-safe bowl, add the blended pineapple mixture. Cover the top of the bowl tightly with plastic wrap. Place the covered bowl over a large pot filled with 3 to 5 inches of water, making sure the bowl doesn't touch the water (you are essentially creating a double boiler). Cook over medium heat for 2 hours. Remove from heat and let cool.

* Yes, I said *canned* pineapple juice! You've heard me wax poetic about the glories of fresh pineapple juice throughout this book, so you may be a little taken aback by the fact that I'm asking you to use canned juice for this syrup. Well, here's why: something about the almost candy-like flavor of canned pineapple juice makes for an absolutely delicious syrup. I've added a little citric acid to this as well to brighten it up a bit and mimic some of the tart notes in fresh pineapple juice. Listen, just trust the process.

MULLED WINE REDUCTION

Makes about 3 cups

1 (750 ml) bottle dry red wine

2 cups (packed) demerara sugar

1 teaspoon vanilla extract

10 whole cloves

2 whole star anise

2 cinnamon sticks

2 dried bay leaves

Combine the red wine and sugar in a large pot. Over medium heat, stir until the sugar has dissolved. Add the vanilla extract, cloves, star anise, cinnamon sticks, and bay leaves and simmer on low heat for 45 minutes to an hour. Remove from heat and let cool to room temperature. Strain through a chinois. Store in a sealed container in the fridge for up to 2 weeks.

SPICED BUTTER

Makes about ½ cup

4 ounces (½ stick) unsalted butter, room temperature

1 tablespoon powdered sugar

1 teaspoon ground cinnamon

¼ teaspoon ground nutmeg

⅛ teaspoon ground cloves

In a bowl, combine the butter, powdered sugar, cinnamon, nutmeg, and cloves and whisk together but don't overmix. The spices should create a swirl and be crudely incorporated for a marbled effect; if the butter turns a solid brown color you have overmixed. Place the butter mixture on a sheet of cellophane. Form into a log with the circumference of a quarter. Refrigerate until it hardens.

CELERY SYRUP

Makes approximately 2 cups
(from about 6 to 8 celery stalks)

200g celery juice

200g white sugar

Combine the celery juice and sugar in a blender and blend until the sugar is dissolved, about 2 to 3 minutes. Store in a sealed container in the fridge for up to 3 days.

Infusions

Each recipe makes 1 (750 ml) bottle

CARAWAY COCCHI AMERICANO

1 (750 ml) bottle Cocchi Americano Bianco

10 grams whole caraway seeds

In a medium pan over medium heat, toast the caraway seeds until fragrant. Combine the toasted seeds with the Cocchi Americano in a sealed container. Let sit for 1 hour. Strain through a chinois. Rebottle and store in the fridge for up to 2 weeks.

JALAPEÑO BLANCO TEQUILA

1 (750 ml) bottle blanco tequila

Seeds of 4 jalapeño peppers*

In a large container, combine the tequila and the jalapeño seeds and let sit for 10 to 15 minutes, tasting periodically, as peppers differ in spice levels. Strain through a chinois. Rebottle and store in fridge for up to 4 weeks.

* Save the flesh of the jalapeño for another use. May I suggest pickling the flesh of the jalapeño and using it as a garnish in your next Martini, Margarita, or salad?

CHAMOMILE BLANC VERMOUTH

1 (750 ml) bottle Dolin Blanc Vermouth

5 grams dried chamomile flowers*

In a large container, combine the vermouth and chamomile flowers and let sit for 30 minutes. Strain through a chinois, making sure to press the liquid out of the flowers. Rebottle and store in fridge for up to 2 weeks.

* Can't find dried chamomile flowers? No problem. Substitute 3 chamomile tea bags.

THAI BASIL BLANC VERMOUTH

100 grams fresh Thai basil leaves, stems removed

1 (750 ml) bottle Dolin Blanc Vermouth

At the bottom of a large container, lightly muddle the basil leaves, making sure to bruise them only slightly to release their oils. Add the blanc vermouth. Let sit for 30 minutes. Strain through a chinois. Rebottle and store in fridge for up to 2 weeks.

SAGE WHITE WINE

10 fresh sage leaves, stems removed

1 (750 ml) bottle dry white wine

At the bottom of a large container, lightly muddle the sage leaves, making sure to bruise them only slightly to release their oils. Add the wine. Let sit for 30 minutes. Strain through a chinois. Rebottle and store in the fridge for up to 5 days.

COLA LUSTAU ROSÉ VERMUT

3 grams cola extract

1 (750 ml) bottle Lustau Rosé Vermut

Add the cola extract to the vermouth bottle. Gently agitate the bottle to combine. Store in the fridge for up to 3 weeks.

BEET APEROL

150 grams beets (about 1 large beet), peeled and diced

1 (750 ml) bottle Aperol

Fill a basin with water and set an immersion circulator to 135°F. Meanwhile, measure the beets by weight. Combine the beets and Aperol in a sealable, heatproof silicone bag, making sure to push out all the air. Once the circulator has reached the desired temperature, place the sealed bag in the water bath. Let cook for 2 hours. Once done, transfer the infusion to an ice bath until it reaches room temperature. Strain through a chinois. Store in a sealed container in the fridge for up to 2 weeks.

No sous vide?
In a large sealable container, combine the beets and Aperol. Cover and let sit at room temperature for 24 hours. Strain through a chinois.

TOASTED COCONUT MADEIRA

50 grams unsweetened coconut chips
1 (750 ml) bottle H&H Rainwater Madeira

Preheat the oven to 350°F. Meanwhile, fill a basin with water and set an immersion circulator to 130°F. Spread the coconut chips on a baking sheet. Toast until fragrant and golden brown, 4 to 5 minutes. Let cool. Combine with the madeira in a sealable, heatproof silicone bag, making sure to push out all the air. Once the circulator has reached the desired temperature, place the sealed bag in the water bath. Let cook for 2 hours. Once done, transfer the infusion to an ice bath until it reaches room temperature. Strain through a cheesecloth-lined chinois. Rebottle and store in the fridge for up to 2 weeks.

No sous vide?
In a large sealable container, combine the toasted coconut chips with the madeira.

Cover and let sit at room temperature for 24 hours. Strain through a cheesecloth-lined chinois. Rebottle and store in the fridge for up to 2 weeks.

CACAO NIB CAMPARI

25 grams cacao nibs
1 (750 ml) bottle Campari

Preheat the oven to 350°F. Meanwhile, fill a basin with water and set an immersion circulator to 130°F. Spread the cacao nibs in a single layer on a baking sheet. Toast until fragrant and dark brown, 3 to 4 minutes. Let cool. Combine with the Campari in a sealable, heatproof silicone bag, making sure to push out all the air. Once the circulator has reached the desired temperature, place the sealed bag in the water bath. Let cook for 2 hours. Once done, transfer the infusion to an ice bath until it reaches room temperature. Strain through a chinois. Rebottle and store in the fridge for up to 2 weeks.

No sous vide?
In a large sealable container, combine the cooled toasted cacao nibs with the Campari. Cover and let sit for 24 hours. Strain through a chinois.

PINEAPPLE MEZCAL

1 (750 ml) bottle Del Maguey Vida mezcal
600 grams chopped fresh pineapple (about 1 medium pineapple)

Fill a basin with water and set an immersion circulator to 140°F. Combine the mezcal and pineapple in a sealable, heatproof silicone bag, making sure to push out all the air. Once the circulator has reached the desired temperature, place the sealed bag in the water bath. Let cook for 2 hours. Once done, transfer the infusion to an ice bath until it reaches room temperature. Strain through a nut bag. Store in a sealed container in the fridge for up to 2 weeks.

No sous vide?
In a large sealable container, combine the mezcal and pineapple. Cover and let sit at room temperature for 72 hours. Strain through a chinois.

A couple of PRO tips here!

- Eat the pineapple post-infusion. Throw it in a punch. Add to a glass of white wine!

- Store this infusion in the freezer and sip on it out of a delicate mini glass from time to time to remind yourself that life is, indeed, good! And we say that since the mezcal has been cut with some pineapple juice, this is relatively low-ABV . . . ish.

VERMOUTH LIMONCELLO

375 ml Cinzano Dry Vermouth

375 ml Cinzano Bianco Vermouth

Peels of 10 lemons

100 grams white sugar

Fill a basin with water and set an immersion circulator to 130°F. Combine the dry vermouth, white vermouth, and lemon peels in a sealable, heatproof silicone bag, making sure to push out all the air. Once the circulator has reached the desired temperature, place the sealed bag in the

water bath. Let cook for 2 hours. Once done, transfer the infusion to an ice bath until it reaches room temperature. Strain through a chinois and discard the peels. In a blender, combine the infused vermouths with the sugar and blend until the sugar has dissolved, 2 to 3 minutes. Store in a sealed container in the fridge for up to 2 weeks.

No sous vide?
In a large sealable container, combine the dry vermouth, white vermouth, and lemon peels. Cover and let sit in the fridge for 72 hours. Strain through a chinois. Discard the peels. In a blender, combine the infused vermouths with the sugar and blend until the sugar is dissolved, 2 to 3 minutes.

CLOVE WHITE PORT

1 (750 ml) bottle Quinta do Infantado white port

8 grams whole cloves

Fill a basin with water and set an immersion circulator to 135°F. Combine the port and cloves in a sealable, heatproof silicone bag, making sure to push out all the air. Once the circulator has reached the desired temperature, place the sealed bag in the water bath. Let cook for 2 hours. Once done, transfer the infusion to an ice bath until it reaches room temperature. Strain through a chinois. Discard the cloves. Store in a sealed container in the fridge for up to 2 weeks.

No sous vide?
In a large sealable container, combine the white port and cloves. Cover and let sit at room temperature for 24 hours. Strain through a chinois, discarding the cloves.

Other Stuff...

SALT SOLUTION

Yield: Approximately ½ cup

100 grams filtered water

30 grams kosher salt

Combine the water and salt in a bowl and whisk until the salt has dissolved. Store in the fridge for up to 1 month. Transfer to a dropper bottle when ready to use.

CITRIC ACID SOLUTION

Yield: Approximately ½ cup

100 grams filtered water

20 grams citric acid powder

Combine the water and citric acid in a bowl and whisk until the citric acid has dissolved. Store in the fridge for up to 1 month. Transfer to bitters dasher bottle when ready to use.

BEFORE YOU GO

Gaskins Garlic Aioli

I want to get back to talking about the French fry really quickly. We can argue over whether we prefer crinkle-cut, waffle, or classic wide-cut fries, but I think we can universally agree that as a category of food, the Fry is a perfect specimen and the ideal bite to accompany any of these cocktails.

I speak frequently of community in this book, so I want to leave you with a gift from my little circle of love and support. It's not a cocktail recipe, but rather, the recipe for the world's most glorious fry sauce. My dear friends Sarah and Nick Suarez own a beautiful restaurant named Gaskins, in Germantown, New York. Years ago, when my husband and I started toying around with the idea of moving to upstate New York, we took a gig helping launch a cocktail program at a hotel in the area. The launch just so happened to coincide with our wedding anniversary, so to celebrate we went to the restaurant that everyone had unanimously recommended. That restaurant was of course Gaskins. And the meal and experience there was so beautiful and impactful that it led to our decision to relocate upstate. Little did I know that Sarah and Nick, who is also the head chef, would become part of our proverbial village.

But back to fries. Gaskins has the best fries! Made even better by their garlic aioli. Generously, they're letting me share this special dipping experience with you. I hope it brings you as much joy as it's brought me and everyone I've ever introduced to Gaskins.

Makes about 2 cups

Garlic Confit and Garlic Oil
1 garlic head
1 cup olive oil

Garlic Aioli
1 whole egg
2 egg yolks
1 tablespoon Dijon mustard
1 tablespoon white wine vinegar
1 whole garlic clove
2 tablespoons water
¾ teaspoon salt
1½ cups canola oil
Zest of ½ lemon

To make garlic confit and garlic oil, first separate and peel all the cloves from the garlic head and place them in a small pot with the olive oil. Bring to a simmer over low heat and cook until the garlic is soft and spreadable but not browned, about 30 minutes. Cool the garlic in the olive oil. The garlic oil will last for up to 2 weeks. Make sure to keep the cooked garlic submerged in the oil.

To make the aioli, add 1 tablespoon of the garlic oil and 2 tablespoons garlic confit, along with the remaining ingredients inside a quart container. Submerge the blade of your immersion blender into the mixture and blend for about 10 seconds. Once the aioli starts to come together, slowly move the immersion blender up and down, blending the mixture until it's completely emulsified. Store, covered, in the refrigerator for up to 1 week.

Even a Cocktail Book Deserves an Epilogue

This book was conceived long before The Event. A proposal was drafted, meetings were held, a contract was signed, cocktails were being tested. My bar, Nitecap, was soaring, basking in the glory of breaking sales records week after week. The month of March 2020 was going to be a big one for the bar. I had saved up enough money to hire a *professional* handyman (I emphasize "professional," because any small business owner will confirm that you usually try to do everything yourself as margins are slim, my friends!) to spruce things up a bit. We were in the thick of menu development for our fourteenth menu edition, and our annual epic staff party was on the books for the end of the month. One week into March, it was business as usual, just with more hand washing and hard-to-come-by hand sanitizer placed throughout the bar. By March fifteenth, two days before the state-mandated shutdown, it started feeling irresponsible to be open. Although the decision wasn't made lightly, we chose to close the bar temporarily in order to ride out whatever this "flu" was. Then of course the whole city got shut down. A few days later, I had laid off my entire staff, cleared out the walk-in, and was sitting alone in my empty, eerily quiet bar feeling entirely lost. Little did I know that March 15, 2020, was going to go down as Nitecap's last night of full service.

In the months that followed, through a combination of factors out of our control, Nitecap, like far too many other bars and restaurants at that time, was forced to close permanently. I quickly came to realize that in the *How to Open a Bar* manual, the chapter titled "How to Close a Bar During a Worldwide Pandemic" had been left out. And let me be the one to tell you that closing a bar felt more draining, time-consuming, and isolating than running a bar. Perhaps because it was filled with so many waves of emotion, consisting mostly of debilitating grief and unfiltered anger. By the end, after having miraculously sold off every last glass and decorative trinket, thanks to a group of loyal Nitecap supporters, I was ready to just retreat into a fuzzy cashmere cocoon and hide with a box of drinkable red, but life's responsibilities kept me moving. Finding the joy was a daily struggle. And after another frustrating afternoon of staring at my computer, trying to come up with something worthy to say for this book, I realized that the reason I was feeling so uninspired was because the closing of Nitecap wasn't just me losing my business; it also signaled the loss of my community. These recipes were more important than ever, and no, I don't have some grandiose delusion that cocktails can bring on world peace. But the very root of this book is the community with whom we chose to share these drinks. And oh my Lord, did I miss my people!

The Event of course was all of our lives being turned upside down by a vicious virus that made the world's glaring inequalities come to a boil all while under soulless leadership. If there's anything The Event made clear, it's our innate need as humans to connect with others, and it is my sincere hope that this book can make your gatherings that much more unified and lively.

Marketplace & Resources

These are some of my most beloved go-to places to shop until I drop. Making delicious and thoughtful drinks starts with sourcing quality ingredients and tools. Hopefully this small but curated list proves to be a solid starting point for your own exploration for cocktail perfection.

Astor Wines & Spirits
astorwines.com
An expansive but carefully selected stock of low-ABV and full-proof spirits. They ship nationwide and saved me on multiple occasions while writing this book in my small town in upstate New York.

Casamara Club
casamaraclub.com
These delicious and complex amaro-inspired sodas will improve your highball game immediately. Of course, they're also delicious on their own.

Chef Shop
chefshop.com
Here you'll find everything from pomegranate molasses to dried spices to exciting sugars. Bonus points for their Women Owned Businesses page.

Cocktail Kingdom
cocktailkingdom.com
So many wonderful and well-designed bar tools!

Dual Specialty Store
dualspecialtystorenyc.com
A tiny, amazing, overflowing basement store filled to the brim with spices, dried herbs, INSPIRATION, and more. A must-visit if you are in New York City.

Kalustyan's
kalustyans.com
You probably can't find a better, bigger, or more awe-inspiring collection of spices, herbs, bitters, nuts, teas, etc., anywhere. Located in New York City, but ships nationwide. Try not to fill your cart with a million things you've never heard of.

Modernist Pantry
modernistpantry.com
If you're looking to become the next molecular gastronomy bartending superstar, then you'll go wild for this site, which has everything from handy gadgets like a Brix meter to all the things you need to make Negroni caviar. I come here for their wide array of different sized superbags, which I know doesn't sound as exciting as Negroni caviar.

SOS Chef
sos-chefs.com
This store is like a fantasy dreamland come to life. Honeys, vinegars, extracts, and more.

Terra Spice Company
terraspice.com
The quality at TS is unrivaled, and I've been a loyal customer for years. It's my go-to for acids, powders, and bulk herbs and spices. Pro tip: Their house ras el hanout blend will make you sing a song of joy.

Umami Mart
umamimart.com
Gorgeous Japanese bar tools, well-stocked bitters selection (including my fave, Miracle Mile), sake, umeshu, glassware, and more. It's a good thing my credit card has a spending limit, because I have a hard time controlling myself here.

Urban Bar
urbanbar.com
Beautiful glassware, bitters bottles, tools, and more. This UK-based company is all about elegance.

My biggest piece of advice when shopping for fun, unique, and festive glassware: shop at your local vintage and thrift stores. You'll most likely find some incredible pieces that are accompanied by colorful and rich history. If you're looking for fresh produce or hard-to-get spices, scour your farmers markets or local Chinatown. Cheers to supporting small and local businesses whenever possible!

Acknowledgments

This book is the culmination of an endless list of people pouring their love, support, and knowledge into me. Putting my gratitude into words seems impossible, but here is my feeble attempt. Never in my wildest dreams would I ever have considered writing a book. Thank you to Ryan Chassee and Zach Greenwald for planting the seed and letting myself imagine this was even a possibility.

I must of course thank "my team." Jonah Straus, my agent, who took a chance on this first-time writer and saw potential in my very incomplete book proposal. Every single person at Clarkson Potter, most especially Jenn Sit, my editor extraordinaire. Thank you for championing and protecting my vision from start to finish. More importantly, my family and I are eternally grateful for your compassion while our world was turned upside down while closing Nitecap. The extension on deadlines meant everything. More heartfelt gratitude to Serena Wang (Production Editor), Ian Dingman (Art Director), Jessica Heim (Production Manager), Bianca Cruz (Editorial Assistant), Samantha Simon and Allison Renzulli (Marketers), and Natalie Yera (Publicist).

Next, I'd love to thank the formidable team that brought these cocktails to life so vibrantly—Kristin Teig (Photographer), Rick Holbrook (Prop Stylist), Molly Corrigan (Prop Stylist Assistant), and Fanny Chu (Food Stylist Assistant). The energy and free-spirited vibez on our little countryside-set allowed us all to take risks—and I think they paid off! And of course, my frequent collaborator Andrés Yeah (Illustrator)—wow, I'm simply blown away by the beauty you create and the imagination living inside you.

Other forces without whom this book wouldn't be what it is: Sean Meagher from Twin Lakes Ice Co. for the gorgeous custom shaped ice blocks, Kathleen Anderson from Hudson Beach Glass for the handblown glassware and glass art. Thank you to the teams at Bacardi, Campari, Forthave Spirits, Good Vodka, Haus Alpenz, KLG PR, Neversink Spirits, Pernod Ricard, Pierre Ferrand, Rosehill Farm, and Skurnik Wines.

There are honestly too many friends to thank, but deep appreciation for the moral support, guidance, and generous care during this process must be sent to Dan Abeles, Lauren Corriveau, Alex Day, David Kaplan, Nathan Oertel, Jessie Paddock, Kallie Robertson, Caroline Snider, Sarah Suarez, and my dad.

To my family and their lineage of kindness I will do my best to carry with me at all times— thank you.

Ma and Alma—you are the idols every human dreams of. I will never not look up to you.

Jeremy—you let me eat your French fries even though I subbed salad on my burger. You are the heartbeat that keeps IT ALL together.

Elliot and Lola— you are the magic that keeps the world spinning. Xoxo

Index

Photographer: Kristin Teig
Prop Stylist: Rick Holbrook
Prop Stylist Assistant: Molly Corrigan
Food Stylist: Natasha David
Food Stylist Assistant: Fanny Chu

Editor: Jennifer Sit
Editorial Assistant: Bianca Cruz
Designer: Ian Dingman
Production Editor: Serena Wang
Production Manager: Jessica Heim
Composition: Merri Ann Morrell
Copy Editor: Anne Cherry
Indexer: Elizabeth Parson

ISBN 978-0-593-23259-0
eISBN 978-0-593-23260-6

Printed in China

10 9 8 7 6 5 4 3 2 1

First Edition